The cover and pages 6 and 80 show details from the 'Rhinebeck' panorama of London, an extraordinarily detailed watercolour drawing on 4 sheets dating from c. 1810. The viewpoint is high in the air over the Pool of London, with the city in the centre and right foreground, Bermondsey and Southwark to the left, and Westminster and the West End in the middle distance.

Lloyd's at Home

The Background and the Buildings

Published for the Corporation of Lloyd's
by Lloyd's of London Press Ltd.
Sheepen Place, Colchester, Essex CO3 3LP

Designed by Theo Hodges, FSIAD FRSA
Printed by William Clowes Ltd,
Beccles, Suffolk
ISBN 1-85044-114-6

Lloyd's at Home

Part One
The Background

Part Two
The Buildings

by
Vanessa Harding
and
Priscilla Metcalf

Lloyd's of London
1986

CLARENCE HOUSE
S.W. 1

I am delighted that the Opening of the
new Lloyd's building is to be marked by the
publication of a book that tells the story of
each building that Lloyd's has occupied and the
history of each site on which that building has
stood - often tracing the tale back to Roman or
pre-Roman times.

The book, I am certain, will not only
entertain but also give us greater insight into
the Society of which I am so happy to be an
Honorary Member.

ELIZABETH R

Queen Mother

Contents

Part One
The Background

by
Vanessa Harding

Chapter One
London,
the
Trading City

From its first existence, London has been known as a port and market. Its location was clearly chosen with this in mind, and for many centuries trade and all its accompanying services centred on the city. Until the late eighteenth century all goods shipped through London had to pass through the city itself, and the Thames was congested with ships from all over the world. Even in the late twentieth century, when the handling of goods has moved elsewhere, and few ships of any size are seen on the river, the city remains the home of marine insurance, financial services, shipping offices and agencies, and commodity trading.

London was founded a few years after the Roman invasion of A.D. 43 – probably around A.D. 50 – and from the first seems to have been a planned commercial settlement. By A.D. 60 Tacitus could describe it as 'a place not indeed distinguished with the title of *colonia*, but crowded with traders and a great centre of commerce'. Archaeological discoveries, both of massive quayside structures and of fine pottery, glass, amphorae of oil and wine, and Mediterranean fruits, dating from the late first and second centuries, testify to the range and importance of London's trade.

Although in the second century trade with the Mediterranean declined, as long as London was part of the Roman empire it shared in a cross-channel trade with other northern provinces. Wares from Gaul and the Rhineland have been found near the waterfront, where the timber quay was extended and rebuilt more than once. Only in the late fourth century, when the barbarian threat was acute, did Londoners choose safety over commercial convenience and build the riverside wall that cut off the city from its quay except for a few access points.

After the departure of the Romans, in the early fifth century, the city was for many years without a major role. The former province was fragmented into many small kingdoms, and urban centres no longer played an important part in the economy. The decaying Roman quays were not suitable for the Saxons, who preferred to beach their flat-bottomed vessels on a strand, and it has been suggested that the focus of early Saxon London lay outside the Roman city to the west, between the Fleet and Aldwych, close to the river.

By the late seventh century, however, London – whether the present city is meant or the western settlement – was recovering some of its urban and commercial functions. Coins of the late seventh century, with the legend 'Londinium', suggest trade and possibly a mint. Around 672 London was described as a port 'where ships come to land', and Bede, writing c. 730, called London 'a mart of many nations coming by land and sea'. Part of the city waterfront was consolidated and reinforced, to provide a hard for drawing up boats, in the late eighth century, and Offa of Mercia (757–96) had diplomatic and trading relations with the Carolingian empire, probably through London, then a Mercian city.

In the ninth century, Viking raids and subsequent full-scale invasions threatened to overwhelm the English kingdoms. London was occupied by the Danes in the early years of Alfred of Wessex's reign; after its recapture in 886, Alfred set about strengthening its defences and encouraging the renewal of urban life. Streets were laid out and, probably, whatever remained of the Roman bridge restored or rebuilt. *Aetheredes hyd*, the landing-place later known as Queenhithe, is mentioned, and there are contemporary references to ships and places to moor them nearby.

In the more settled conditions of the first half of the tenth century, London continued to grow. Billingsgate, the other main city wharf, is referred to around the year 1000, when merchants of northern France, Flanders, and Germany came there with goods of many kinds. Renewed Danish attacks on the city, and their final conquest of it and the rest of England, did not seriously damage its development. Indeed, once Danish

The centre of the city and the northern suburb of London c. 1553–9; the two surviving plates of the 'Copperplate Map'.

and Norse domination of the north sea coasts was complete, and London came within that sphere, trade may even have been encouraged.

The Norman conquest of England and the continued links with northern and western France through the Angevin dynasty and the accession of the duchy of Aquitaine put London at the centre of trade routes stretching north and south. In the late twelfth century, St. Thomas Becket's biographer, writing about the saint's native city, claimed that London received Arab gold, spices and incense, palm oil, jewels, Chinese cloths, French wines, and Russian sables. The city functioned as an entrepôt rather than as a producer of goods, since the principal exports of England were food and raw materials, particularly, by the thirteenth century, wool, which went to the cloth-producing centres of Ghent, Ypres, and Bruges in the Low Countries.

By the fourteenth century the whole waterfront of the city, from Blackfriars to the Tower, was built up and out into numerous private wharves and landing stages. Local and foreign goods were landed at these and at Queenhithe and Billingsgate; wine from Gascony was landed at the wharves in the Vintry, and wool was customed and loaded at the Woolwharf, later Custom House Quay. At the same time there were many watergates and stairs through which Londoners had access to the river for water, washing, swimming, and the disposal of rubbish. In the 1390s several hundred ships visited London every year, many of them small vessels from the Low Countries but including the great ships of the Hanse, Venetian galleys, and Genoese cogs.

It was during the fourteenth century that English cloth production began to expand, taking over first the home market, formerly supplied at least in part by Flemish merchants, and in the fifteenth century ousting wool as England's principal export. London had an increasingly large share of the cloth export trade: by the sixteenth century over four-fifths of all English cloth exports went through London. These were principally unfinished or partly finished cloths for the Low Countries, where cloth-finishing was taking the place of cloth-weaving. The most important commercial axis of the mid sixteenth century was that between London and Antwerp, and in return for its cloth exports London received manufactured and exotic goods for distribution throughout England.

Even when the Antwerp axis was broken, with the Dutch Revolt and Spanish retaliation, the export of woollen cloth to European markets remained the most important element in English trade. The late sixteenth century saw the creation of new chartered companies with the aim of exploiting opportunities for expansion, finding new goods or new markets. The early seventeenth century, beginning with peace with France and Spain, saw an expansion of trade, but also a change in emphasis. The older trade in heavy English cloth, with northern and western Europe, was gradually overtaken by the export of the 'New Draperies' – lightweight and fancy cloths – which sold much better in southern Europe. So far, the new colonies had not provided much of a market for English cloth.

In 1640, 80 to 90% of London's exports were woollen textiles: some 86,000 traditional 'shortcloths', and over £450,000 worth of other textiles and hosiery, including the New Draperies. At the same time, however, the re-export trade was growing in importance, and it was this, the traffic in foreign goods to foreign destinations, that was to be the expanding sector of English overseas trade in the later seventeenth century. By that time the American and Indian colonies were producing cheaply new commodities – tobacco, sugar, coffee, calico – which found a wide market in England and Europe.

The late-seventeenth-century expansion of trade resulted in several new developments in London. In the first place, there were new commodities for sale, and new shops sprang up to sell them. Confectioners, tobacconists, 'coffee-men', occur in London in the 1660s, and increasingly thereafter.

Secondly, while marine insurance had long been known in London, introduced by the sophisticated Italian merchants of the fifteenth century, there was now a much greater need for it, with more ships, longer voyages, greater risks, greater profits. There was also a larger business community, with more available capital and better book-keeping and accounting practices. It was in these circumstances that the coffee-house developed, as a useful centre for the exchange of information and, as time went on, specialised dealing of one sort or another. The coffee-house Edward Lloyd opened in Tower Street in or before 1687 was not the first, but it was to be the most famous.

Since that time, the appearance of the city has changed enormously, but it has not changed beyond recognition. Although industrial, technological, and political revolutions have fundamentally reshaped the world, it is still possible to feel that the city, and particularly its eastern half, is a city of the late seventeenth and early eighteenth centuries. The character it has now was acquired then, when the institutions of finance and world trade settled there. It is still possible to understand what the city of that date was physically like; we still have the same terms of reference, the early medieval street-plan and layout, and some of the churches, to guide us.

Woodcut view of the city from the south, showing St. Paul's Cathedral as it was before the spire was destroyed in 1561.

Chapter Two
Lime Street before Lloyd's 1

London around A.D. 125, a reconstruction by Alan Sorel. The city is seen from the south-east, with the basilica and forum in the centre and the fort at Cripplegate beyond.

Tessellated pavement found in Leadenhall Street
in 1803, in front of East India House, which stood
on the site now occupied by Lloyd's.

Chapter Two
Lime Street before Lloyd's

It is possible to trace the histories of some of the properties on the sites now occupied by Lloyd's through documents back to the twelfth century. Using archaeological evidence, some idea of the character of the area in the Roman period can be given. The story that emerges, as well as being informative about the site itself, illustrates many events and movements in the history of the city and the country.

Roman London

The focus of Roman London was Cornhill, the eastern of the two hills on which the settlement was founded. There was probably a market-place here from the first, but the earliest buildings recovered date from the late first century, after the Boudiccan fire of A.D. 61. The early basilica and forum straddled what is now Gracechurch Street; the Lloyd's site lies just to the east of this. Together they measured some 104 m. by 52 m., and there was a temple or temples nearby. To the south of this area the slope down to the river was terraced, and a massive quay built.

A second and larger forum and basilica, overlying the first but measuring some 167 m. square, were built in the early second century, possibly to commemorate the visit of the Emperor Hadrian in A.D. 122. The basilica was probably the largest building in Roman Britain, but it was burnt, with much of the rest of the city, in the 'Hadrianic' fire of A.D. 125/130.

Though much of the city was rebuilt after this second fire, by the later second century the settlement may have been beginning to contract. Archaeological evidence presents a paradox: certainly some formerly occupied areas and buildings were abandoned, but at the same time some massive public works, particularly along the waterfront, were undertaken, and the landward city wall was built. Some of the finest private dwellings also date from the second and third centuries, and demonstrate that a wealthy and civilised lifestyle was available, at least for some.

Tessellated or mosaic floors have been excavated in many places in the city; one of the finest of these, probably more than 20 m. square, was

(Below left) Head of Hadrian found in the Thames. *(Below right)* Tessellated pavement found in Leadenhall Street during the demolition of East India House in 1858–9.

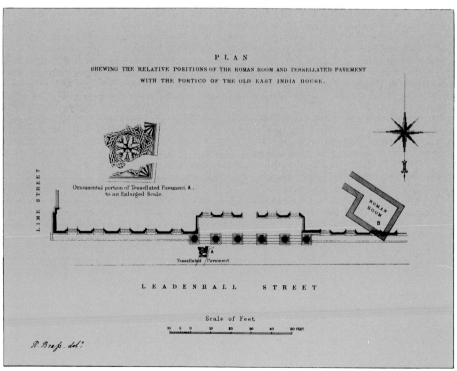

PLAN
SHEWING THE RELATIVE POSITIONS OF THE ROMAN ROOM AND TESSELLATED PAVEMENT
WITH THE PORTICO OF THE OLD EAST INDIA HOUSE.

LIME STREET

Ornamental portion of Tessellated Pavement. A. to an Enlarged Scale.

ROMAN ROOM B

Tessellated Pavement

LEADENHALL STREET

Scale of Feet

R. Brass. del.

discovered in Leadenhall Street in front of East India House in 1803. The centrepiece showed Bacchus on a panther; though the floor was damaged by its removal, part of it survives in the British Museum. Other such pavements were found in Leadenhall Street later in the nineteenth century, mostly during demolition and building works. Usually the contexts of such discoveries – remains of buildings, walls, foundations – were not recorded, so it is difficult to determine the layout of the area.

Twentieth-century excavations have been more careful as to context, and the remains of buildings in Lime Street (found before the 1950s building was erected) and Leadenhall Street have been carefully planned. The wider context, however, the street-plan of the city, is still open to reinterpretation; excavations in 1983 and 1984 at Cullum Street, at the south end of Lime Street, are revealing more about the line of the street running eastwards from the southern end of the forum, and may help to determine the alignment of buildings and foundations further north.

Coin hoards from Lime Street, and elsewhere in the city, have been taken as evidence of the external threat to the city in the late third century. A pot

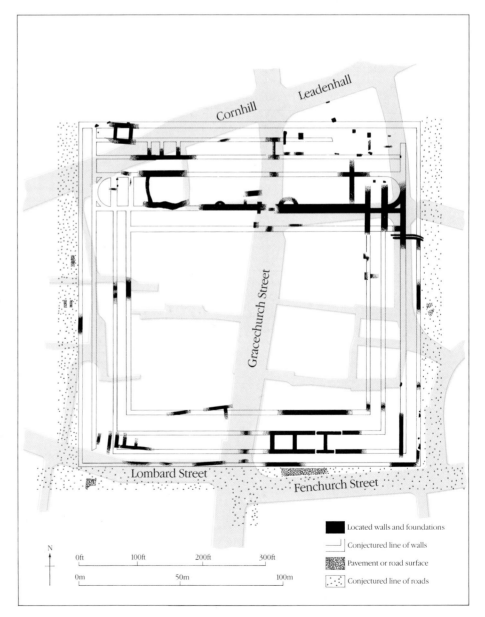

Plan of the second-century forum and basilica, overlaid on the modern street-plan. This reconstruction, based on the evidence of two centuries of building works and archaeological excavation, may have to be modified when excavations begun in 1985 at the north end of Gracechurch Street are complete.

containing 500 denarii of silver and other metals, found in Lime Street in 1882, was deposited in or after A.D. 249–50, and subsequently forgotten. Nevertheless city life continued, even if on a less grand scale. Excavations in Lime Street in 1951 found a Roman building with stone walls, plain red mosaic pavements, and heated rooms. It was enlarged in the late third century, but seems to have been destroyed by fire in the mid fourth century. London was attacked by the Saxons in 367–8, and though Theodosius was sent to strengthen the city – it was probably in his time that the bastions and the riverside wall were built – Roman London had not long to live.

The Roman administration in Britain collapsed in the early fifth century, with the withdrawal of the legions. The settled, organised urban life characteristic of Roman civilisation declined and surviving Roman buildings decayed or were abandoned. Only the city's well-chosen site, its defensive walls, its name and reputation, ensured its continued existence in some form, even when the fundamental conditions of political life and economic activity had changed.

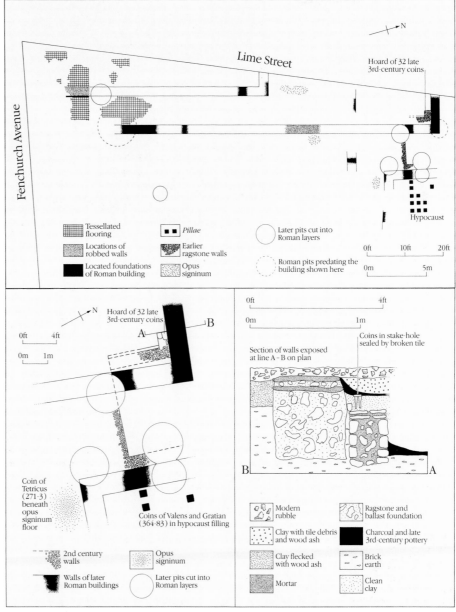

(Above) Gold medallion commemorating the arrival of Constantinus Chlorus in London in A.D. 296.

(Right) Plan and section of excavations of a late Roman building on the east side of Lime Street in 1951. The site was cut into by later medieval rubbish pits, but foundations, areas of red tesserae, and some opus signinum (a distinctive pinkish mortar made with crushed pottery) remained.

17

Roman Remains

(Right) Public interest in a Roman pavement excavated in Poultry near the Mansion House in 1869. Road- and building-works in London in the nineteenth century led to a number of exciting discoveries.

(Centre) Coin of Diocletian (A.D. 284–305), minted in London in 297.

(Below) Roman and medieval foundations and wall exposed during the building of Leadenhall Market in 1881–2. The walls in the right foreground probably represent part of the forum and basilica complex.

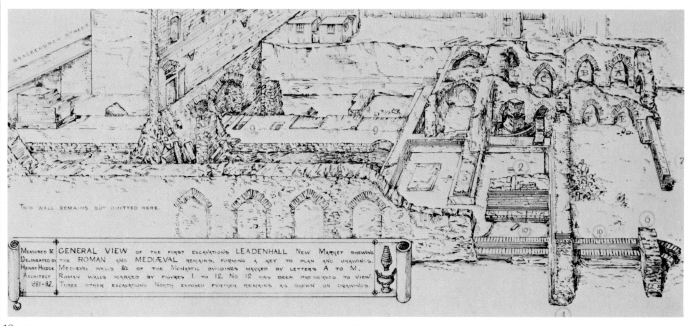

Dark Age and Saxon London

The settlers who succeeded the Romans in London left no traces in the area now under consideration. In many parts of the city there are no occupation layers between the Roman and the medieval, and much of the city area seems to have been depopulated and abandoned.

When urban life within the walls revived in the ninth century, the Roman street plan had been almost completely lost, apart from the access points through the wall dictated by the Roman gates. Even the street running down from Bishopsgate to the bridge takes a different line from the Roman street doing the same, and cuts across the middle of the forum. After his conquest of London from the Danes in 886, King Alfred 'refurbished the walls, repopulated the city, and... assigned to various magnates plots of land bounded by streets'. It is probable that he created the irregular grid of streets covering the western half of the city, around Cheapside, and the south-eastern part near Eastcheap; it is noticeable that the Lime Street area stands apart from this.

In the tenth and eleventh centuries London grew in size and wealth. By the time of the Norman conquest the city had several mints, a number of churches besides St. Paul's, a popular assembly and a public court. The population may still have been concentrated in the western half of the city and the western suburb towards Westminster, however, and it is not until the twelfth century that we know anything of Lime Street.

Saxon London, showing the irregular grid of streets that may have been laid out by Alfred (871–899).

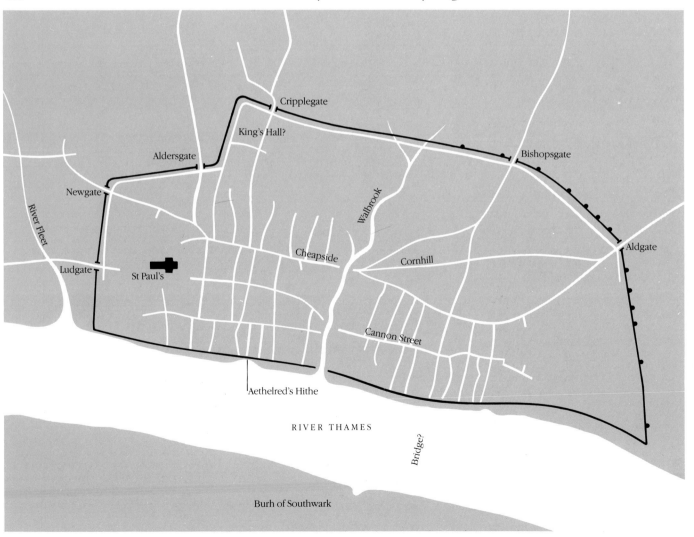

The Medieval Period

In the two centuries following the Norman Conquest, London acquired most of the features which distinguished it in the medieval period. The sheriffs, the mayor, and the governing bodies of aldermen and commoners developed, even if they had not reached their final form; courts and distinctive legal procedures evolved; the hundred-odd parish churches, and several of the monasteries and hospitals were established; a new stone bridge was built across the river; and the population of the city grew to fill much of the walled area and some of the suburbs.

In Lime Street, as elsewhere in the city, there was a complete break in the topographical arrangement between the Roman and early medieval periods, but the pattern of streets and properties that had been established by the twelfth and thirteenth centuries endured into the eighteenth, ninetheenth, and even twentieth centuries.

The first appearance of the name Lime Street (as *Limstrate*) and the first records of landowners and inhabitants there date from the 1170s and 1180s.

London *c.* 1200. By this date most of the city's churches and monasteries had been founded, the street pattern was clear, and the bridge had been rebuilt.

St Bartholomew's Priory

Jews' Cemetery

Cripplegate

THE MOOR

St Bartholomew's Hospital

Aldersgate

Aldermanbury

Bishopsgate

Bishopsgate Street

St Martin's le Grand

Guildhall?

Holy Trinity Priory

PORTSOKEN

Jewry

St Andrew

St Paul's

Folkmoot

West Cheap

Corn Hill

Aldgate

Bishop's Palace

Lime Street

The Vintry

Candlewick Street

East Cheap

East Smithfield

RIVER THAMES

The Tower

St Katharine's Hospital

Priory of St Mary Overy

SOUTHWARK

Written records relating to city property before that period are very sparse, and it is likely that the street had existed, and perhaps been known by that name, some time earlier. In this quarter of the city the grid-plan, which may reflect King Alfred's laying-out of streets and plots in the ninth century, is absent, or was overlaid at an early date. Lime Street is probably later than the grid, and its double bend suggests the possibility that there were large or important properties in Leadenhall Street and Fenchurch Street which a street joining the two had to bypass. The bend remained even when all trace of the former properties which caused it had disappeared.

The name Lime Street probably meant 'street where lime was burned or sold'. Ailnoth *calcerius* (the lime-burner) held land near here in the early thirteenth century, and it is possible that the late-twelfth-century Fulcred de Limstrate is the same as Fulcred Limbernarius who occurs in records of the same time. Even if lime was only sold and not burned here (no reference to lime-kilns has been found), the area was probably not very built up yet, since lime is a bulky commodity to store and handle. Its chief use at this date was in mortar and plaster. At a later date lime was burned outside the city, as the name Limehouse (lime-oasts) indicates.

The church of St. Andrew, now called Undershaft but for long known as St. Andrew Cornhill, is first recorded in the twelfth century, though it could

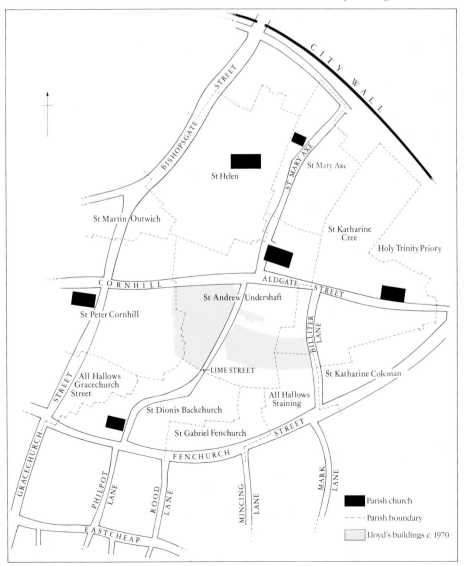

(Above) Reverse of the early medieval seal of the city of London. It shows St. Thomas Becket, born in London, enthroned above the skyline of the city, encircled by a prayer: 'Cease not, Thomas, to guard me who brought thee forth'.
(Right) Plan of the streets and parishes round Lime Street as they were from the early Middle Ages to the nineteenth century. The positions of Cooper's and Heysham's buildings for Lloyd's are in colour.

(Above) Obverse of the city's seal, showing St. Paul, with sword and banner, above the walls and towers of London.
(Below) An imaginative nineteenth-century engraving of celebrations round the maypole in front of the church of St. Andrew Undershaft.

have existed earlier. Nothing survives of the earliest church building; as it now stands it is mostly of sixteenth-century date. The base of the tower is the oldest part of the church, and dates from the fifteenth century, but the upper part of the tower was rebuilt in the nineteenth century. The sixteenth-century rebuilding of the church, and its benefactors, are described in Chapter III.

Because there were so many churches in the city, it was necessary to distinguish ones with the same dedication by adding a surname. Some of these surnames refer to location, some to the founder, some to a notable feature of the church or its surroundings. There were three other churches dedicated to St. Andrew the Apostle: St. Andrew Hubbard, in Eastcheap, now lost, St. Andrew at Baynard's Castle, now called St. Andrew by the Wardrobe, and St. Andrew Holborn. The surname 'Cornhill' is a reminder that the street now called Leadenhall Street was in the Middle Ages known as Cornhill for about as far east as the church. From the church eastwards to Aldgate it was known as Aldgate Street. St. Andrew's was also called St. Andrew within Aldgate, and St. Andrew by Christchurch. 'Christchurch' was the name by which Londoners knew the priory of Holy Trinity within Aldgate, which lay where Duke's Place now is; St. Katharine Cree (= Creechurch or Christchurch) takes its surname from the same priory.

In the fifteenth century the church was called St. Andrew 'atte Knappe', this being, it is thought, the knob or mound in the street in which the maypole kept near the church was set. The later fifteenth and sixteenth century names of 'atte Shaft' or Undershaft refer to the maypole itself; Chaucer mentions the 'great shaft of Cornhill'. According to the antiquary John Stow, the great maypole was never used again after the May-day riot of 1517 ('Evil May Day'), but hung up under the eaves of the houses on the north side of Leadenhall Street. In 1549 a fervent Protestant preacher denounced the maypole as idolatrous, and the tenants of the houses where it hung, filled with enthusiasm, took it down and sawed it up, dividing the bits between them. Shaft Alley or Court on the north side of the street took its name from the pole.

The former parish of St. Andrew Cornhill or Undershaft centred on the crossroads in front of the church, extending westwards along Leadenhall Street towards Gracechurch Street, eastwards nearly to Billiter Street, southwards down Lime Street as far as the lane that leads into Leadenhall Market, and northwards a little way beyond the church. Virtually the whole of the buildings now occupied by Lloyd's in Lime Street lie within the old parish, except for the eastern end of the eastern building, which is in the parish of St. Katharine Cree.

The street called St. Mary Axe, north of Leadenhall Street, takes its name from a lost parish church which stood towards the northern end of the street, and which was closed in 1562, probably because of the poverty or scarcity of its parishioners. The parish of St. Mary Axe was added to that of St. Andrew, and the old church building was let for secular use. The church of St. Mary Axe had a subsidiary dedication to St. Ursula, and had as a sacred relic an axe, reputedly the axe with which St. Ursula and the Eleven Thousand Virgins were martyred. Another local landmark in the Middle Ages and later was Leadenhall. This was a large house or hall, probably with a leaden roof, dating from the late thirteenth century or earlier, and standing near the corner of Leadenhall Street (as it became) and Gracechurch Street. It stood on a large property owned in the twelfth century by the de Cornhill family and from 1195 by the Nevilles. By the late fourteenth century the property was edged with rows of shops facing the street; in the 1980s the back wall of some of the street-front buildings was found to incorporate part of the wall of Leadenhall itself. There was also a chapel attached to the hall, rebuilt in the fifteenth century, which survived until 1812.

Even in the fourteenth century, when it was still a private property,

Medieval Trades

The inhabitants of medieval cities carried on a wide range of trades and crafts; a London list of 1423 names one hundred and eleven. These illustrations, from a variety of sources, show: cloth-dyeing; weaving; a herbalist; the minting of coins; and the preparation of medicines.

Leadenhall was used as a market for country poulterers. It was acquired by the city in 1411 and substantially rebuilt between 1440 and 1455. It was used both as a fresh produce market and for storing goods: tanned leather was sold there, the city used parts of it for a granary and an arsenal, and the Merchants of the Staple, wool exporters, rented the chapel, for use as a warehouse, from 1479. The poultry market held here seems to have attracted poulterers to some of the houses and shops along Leadenhall Street.

The history of the properties occupying what is now the Lloyd's site in the Middle Ages is full of interest. Written records survive from the late twelfth century, though they are not plentiful until the fourteenth. From then on, however, it is possible to trace in detail the histories of individual houses or holdings, and even in some cases to locate them on a map or plan. Details of what the buildings were like inside or outside occur rarely before the sixteenth century, but enough is known about medieval urban development to suggest parallels.

The histories of individual properties illustrate many important aspects of city life. The impact of external events – the Black Death, the Wars of the Roses – was also felt here. Perhaps the first point brought out in writing the histories of the Lloyd's site properties is that we owe our earliest understanding of landholding in London to the records of monastic houses. No private person in the eleventh and twelfth centuries was keeping (and successfully preserving) records of the acquisition and disposal of property as monasteries did. The earliest landowners we know of in the Lime Street

The north front of Leadenhall, with the main gate. The engraving dates from the seventeenth or eighteenth century but appears to show the building as it was rather earlier.

The Front of Leaden-Hall.

area, therefore, are the abbey of Ramsey in Huntingdonshire and the priory of Holy Trinity within Aldgate in London, to the east of Lime Street, and Bermondsey Priory to the west. These lands were occupied by tenants, who in time came to be almost freeholders, owing only a nominal rent to their ecclesiastical landlords.

The twelfth- and early thirteenth-century property records suggest that the Lime Street area, though divided into separate plots, some of which had substantial stone houses on them, was still spacious. Certainly it was not as densely settled and built up as Cheapside, the heart of the city, was at this date. Gardens and even an orchard are mentioned, and gardens and yards remained in evidence until the eighteenth century.

By the early fourteenth century the commercial character of the area was becoming apparent. It was common for craftsmen and retailers in the same trade to congregate in a single locality, and by 1300 the predominant trade of the landholders along the Leadenhall Street frontage was that of potter. At this time a potter (*pottarius, ollarius*) was a maker of metal pots, not a worker in clay. His main occupation would be making the cast-metal pots and cauldrons used for cooking and for industrial purposes: many manufacturing processes (brewing, dyeing, candlemaking) involved heating or boiling over a fire.

The potters were also the bellmakers of medieval London. Richard de Wymbush, potter, who lived in a house on this site (p.29) cast two bells for Holy Trinity Priory, the smaller of which, cast in 1312, weighed over a ton.

Leadenhall Chapel, built in the fifteenth century, shown *c.* 1805, shortly before its demolition.

Bellmaking in the City

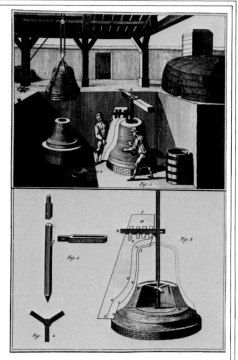

Stages in bellmaking, from illustrations of bell-foundries of the sixteenth, eighteenth, and nineteenth centuries.

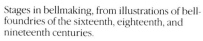

Bellmaking took place in Leadenhall Street in the early fourteenth century, but later moved out to the eastern suburbs. This bell was cast by Robert Mot of Whitechapel in 1573. Four of his bells hung in St. Andrew Undershaft in 1929.

Billiter Street, formerly Billiter Lane, means the lane of the bellmakers or 'bell-yetters'. Another inhabitant c. 1300, Robert de Algate, also had land in the suburb without Aldgate, where several more potters and bellmakers are found in the fourteenth and fifteenth centuries. So too did Robert Burford (p.38), one of the few actually to call himself 'bellfounder'. It seems probable that metalworking and perhaps bellmaking were taking place in this part of Leadenhall Street in the early fourteenth century, but that by the fifteenth century, following the tendency for 'noisome' or unpleasant trades to be pushed out to the suburbs, these activities were probably being practised elsewhere. Bellmaking continued in Whitechapel until the twentieth century.

The Black Death struck London with terrible force in 1348. The city, busy, crowded, an international port, with a population of more than 50,000, may have lost a third or more of its population. Between October 1348 and December 1349 the wills of 361 citizens (the upper layer of society, the property-owners) were proved and enrolled in the city's Court of Husting. The average number proved in a period of that length before 1348 was 35 or 40. Many of these wills were brief and hurriedly made; many of those named as legatees in one will themselves appear as testators within a few weeks. Several of the Leadenhall Street property-owners died in the Plague, and often, if all their immediate family died out, it is difficult to trace how their property passed to its next owner.

Subsequent epidemics of plague in 1361, 1369, and 1375, though less severe, effectively prevented a significant recovery in population levels, and in the later fourteenth and fifteenth centuries the city was emptier, of people and of standing houses, than for many decades before 1300. With a lower population and a reduced market – London's most important function was as a centre for consumption and redistribution – the value of city property fell. Rents began to fall in many parts of the city, and houses and shops surplus to the present population's requirements were abandoned or pulled down. There are fewer records of property-holding in the fifteenth century, and it becomes difficult or impossible to trace the histories of several properties.

As well as the citizen craftsmen and retailers who occupied parts of the Lloyd's site, several noble or knightly families owned land there, mostly the back lands behind the commercial frontage, where there was room for substantial houses. Pembridge's Inn and Tiptoft's mansion were two of these. The descent of such properties illustrates aspects of the life of the gentry, in particular their involvement, often fatal, in the fifteenth-century wars in France and England. The descendants of Sir John Tiptoft fought on opposite sides in the Wars of the Roses.

Popular unrest also had its impact on the area. In 1449 Cade's rebels attacked Sheriff Philip Malpas's house (p.32), and in 1517 rioting apprentices attacked the house occupied by the Frenchman John Meautis (p.30). The Crown's interest in city property becomes apparent: when a house, such as the Green Gate, came into its hands, it could be used as a reward for service, and granted, for life or permanently, to a retainer or, very often, a personal servant or member of the royal household.

As well as the private owners of land, there were institutional ones. As we have seen, religious houses are the earliest known holders of land in this area, and in fact more than a hundred such houses (abbeys, priories, friaries, hospitals) had city property in the Middle Ages. This served as a source of income, in the same way that farms and manors did; in some cases the abbot or prior also used a property as a London residence. Such endowments usually derived from gifts or bequests, not from purchase.

In the fourteenth and fifteenth centuries popular piety turned towards founding chantries and masses for the dead rather than endowing monasteries and nunneries. Many London parish churches were left houses or lands, to provide an income for the chantry priest or to pay for special services and prayers for the benefactor. Any residue of income might be directed to be spent on repairs to the church, or distributed in bread and cash to the poor.

At the same time, the fraternities and craft guilds which Londoners had been forming since at least the thirteenth century were growing into the Livery Companies of today. As well as controlling the exercise of particular trades, and entrance to the freedom of the city, they had a social and often a religious function. Members left them property to maintain chantries and anniversary masses, and to support poor members of the craft, as well as simply to enlarge and enrich the body to which they belonged. The Companies grew in wealth and splendour, acquiring royal charters and building themselves grand halls where they could dine and celebrate in state.

The Reformation had a great impact on landholding in the city. In the first place, with Henry VIII's dissolution of the monasteries, which mostly took place between 1536 and 1540, a great deal of land, in the city and elsewhere, came into the Crown's possession. Then, in 1548, the strongly Protestant council of Edward VI declared all chantries and obituary masses to be superstitious and without spiritual value, and confiscated all lands and endowments used to support them. This included some of the lands held by the Livery Companies. The London lands that came into the Crown's hands through these two events rapidly came onto the market again, being bought from the Crown by speculators and land-dealers and sold again to Londoners.

In the property histories which follow, those to the west of Lime Street are taken first, starting, after a brief introduction, with the westernmost property forming part of what is now the Lloyd's site, and continuing eastwards and then southwards down Lime Street. The properties east of Lime Street follow. In describing locations, the modern names 'Leadenhall Street' and 'St. Andrew Undershaft' are used, for simplicity, but deeds and contemporary references usually say "Cornhill' and 'St. Andrew Cornhill' or 'atte Knappe'.

The Properties: West of Lime Street

The history of the properties on the west side of Lime Street in the twelfth and early thirteenth centuries is not known. The great property of the Neville family, most of which subsequently became Leadenhall, may once have included lands extending as far as Lime Street, but by the mid thirteenth century the properties bordering Lime Street were held as several different units. On the corner of Lime Street and Leadenhall Street there were several houses and gardens, once belonging to Bermondsey Priory, but by 1278 held by William Grapefige, a spice-dealer. These houses were enclosed to the west and south by a single property (a dwelling-house and garden) belonging to Arnulf le Bret.

The southernmost property of those on what is now the Lloyd's site belonged to Eudo la Zouche (d. 1279), and was probably held after his death by his widow Millicent, usually known as Millicent de Mohaut or de Monte Alto, from her first husband, John de Mohaut. In the 1280s she acquired properties to the north of the one she already held, and in Leadenhall Street, and probably ended up with a large L-shaped block of property opening onto both Leadenhall Street and Lime Street. This property passed, probably before Millicent's death in 1299, to Robert de Algate, potter. He also acquired the le Bret property already mentioned, and another plot further west on Leadenhall Street.

By the early fourteenth century there were four main property blocks on the Lloyd's site west of Lime Street, and one in Lime Street. The history of each of these properties is given below.

The Green Gate

The property to the west of Robert de Algate's lay partly in the parish of St. Andrew Undershaft (in which all the other properties lay) and partly in the parish of St. Peter Cornhill, and was bounded to the south by properties belonging to the de Neville family and to Robert de Algate. In 1313 Richard de Wymbush, potter, sold it to another potter, William de Algate. William sold it to Henry in the Lane, potter, in 1318, but probably continued to live there, and bought it back from Henry's executors in 1335. In 1340 William and his wife Margaret granted the property to Thomas Meel, hatter.

The property's descent through the period of the Black Death (1348–9) is not clear, but by 1353 it belonged to William de Berking and Robert de Thame, fishmongers, who then granted it to Simon of Pistoia, a Lombard who had taken out London citizenship, and was a dealer in spices and medicinal drugs. He was also known as Simon Pistoye or Lespicer. At this time there were many naturalised Italians living in London, usually involved like Simon in the spice and drug trade, or in importing silk and fine fabrics. Simon died

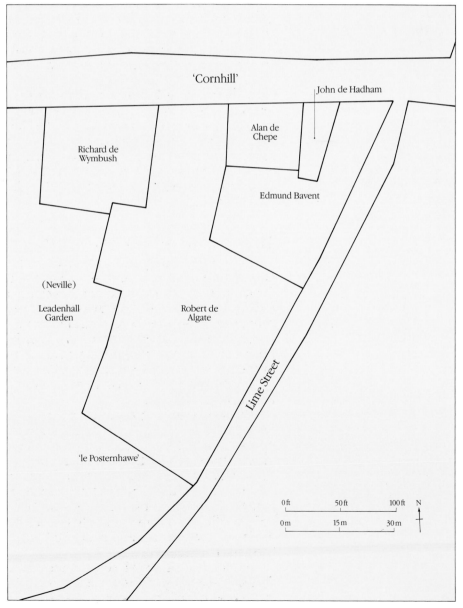

Plan of the properties to the west of Lime Street, c. 1300. The large property held at this date by Robert de Algate was subsequently broken up. This plan and the following ones were drawn on a scaled base, with as much accuracy as possible, but some of the detail is inevitably conjectural. The relationships between properties should be right, but the exact location of boundaries may be uncertain.

around 1360, but his wife Emma continued to hold the property till 1390, when she sold it. On her death in 1391, however, the King claimed the property, because Simon had no heirs living. It is at this date that the property is first recorded by the name of *Le Grenegate*, presumably in reference to an actual green gate or door there. The situation was resolved in 1408, when those who had purchased the Green Gate from Emma resigned all their claim to Thomas Walsingham, to whom the King had granted it.

Thomas Walsingham's family still held this property in 1462. By 1486 it was again in the King's possession, and was granted for life to his servant John Alston. Alston forfeited the property for failing to attend Henry VII's expedition against the Cornish rebels in 1497, and the Green Gate was granted temporarily to Humphrey Dore, chief purveyor to the Butlery. It was next held by William de la Ryver, and in 1507 Henry VII granted it to his 'secretary for the French tongue', John Meautis.

By this time the property comprised the main dwelling, four other houses, probably all separately occupied, two cellars, and a garden. John Meautis was fortunate to be absent from home on 1 May 1517, when the apprentices' traditional May-day celebration turned into a riot in which the houses of many foreigners were attacked. Meautis was suspected of housing and protecting Frenchmen who were engaged in clothworking, contrary to the citizens' privileges: 'the Prentizes and other spoyled his house; and if they

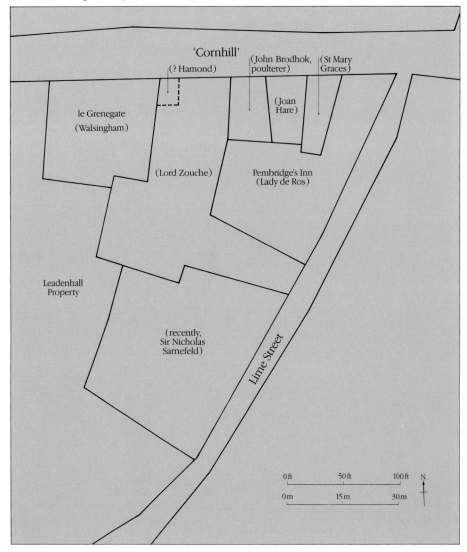

Plan of the properties west of Lime Street, *c.* 1400.

could have found (him) they would have stricken off his heade' (John Stow). 'Evil May Day', as the riot came to be called, was long remembered in the city.

Robert de Algate's property

In the early fourteenth century, Robert de Algate held a very large property with a frontage both to Leadenhall Street and to Lime Street. Before his death, in or before 1347, he had begun to divide it up (see p.36).

A small property on Leadenhall Street, between the Green Gate on the west and the main part of Robert de Algate's property on the east and south, belonged to Robert de Algate at one time but was subsequently detached to form a separate property. In 1363 it was held by John Clapschethe, poulterer, who sold it to John Toot, draper, who then granted it to Adam Hamond. In all these transactions the property is referred to as a *mansio*, meaning a dwelling-house, perhaps one of some size. In 1422 it was acquired by William Traynell, citizen, who was living there in 1431 and probably on his death in 1436. In 1439 his trustees sold it, with his widow's agreement, to Stephen Broun, grocer and alderman for Aldgate ward. Broun became mayor later in 1439, and again in 1448–9. It is not certain that he lived in this house, but if he did it was probably in the period of his first mayoralty. He died between 1462 and 1466, leaving this property among others to his son

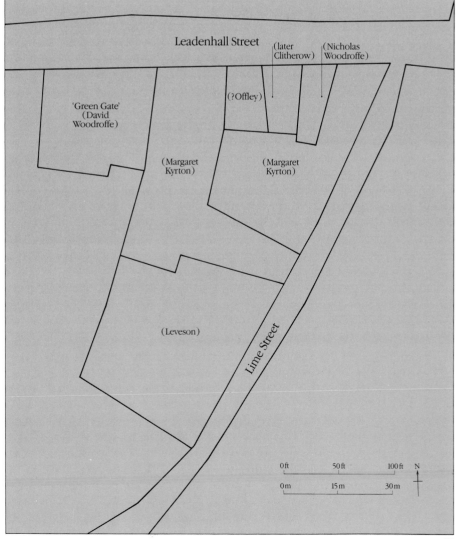

Plan of the properties west of Lime Street, *c.* 1560.

Thomas and his male heirs: the descent after this date is uncertain.

After granting away the southern part of his property in Lime Street, Robert de Algate probably kept the rest as one unit until his death in or before 1347. This then passed to his son Thomas, who died between 1347 and 1349, probably in the Black Death. It is not certain what happened next, but by 1358 the property was held by William Lord Zouche of Haryngworth. This William was the great-grandson of Eudo la Zouche and Millicent de Mohaut, who had held at least part of the property before Robert de Algate, and possibly he was able to claim it as his inheritance when Robert's heirs died out.

When William died in 1382 he held two houses and seven shops in Lime Street ward, worth £6 13s. 4d. yearly. His son William, third Lord Zouche of Haryngworth, inherited it; when he died in 1396 it was valued at £2 0s. 9d. yearly. When his son William, fourth Lord Zouche, died in 1415, the property, now described as an inn or hospice (meaning a noble residence), was worth only £2 yearly. The fall in demand for property, reflected by falling rent values, also meant that there were fewer records of property kept by the mid-fifteenth century. There are no deeds relating to this large property, and its descent can only be inferred from occasional references.

After the fourth Lord Zouche's death in 1415, the property probably passed out of that family. In 1462 Philip Malpas held it, and he was probably living here as early as 1449, when he was sheriff, when Jack Cade's rebels attacked his house. At some time in the later fifteenth century it was held by Sir Philip Coke, kt. It seems to have been granted (by whom is not known) to the rector and churchwardens of St. Andrew Undershaft to maintain a chantry. As a 'superstitious' endowment it was forfeited to the Crown in 1548, and sold later that year to Thomas White and Stephen Kyrton, two leading citizens and aldermen.

John de Hadham's properties

On Leadenhall Street (referred to in deeds as Cornhill) there were two, later three, small properties between Robert de Algate's to the west and the corner property on Lime Street, later called Pembridge's Inn, to the east and south. All the properties may once have belonged to the le Bret family, but by the early fourteenth century the western one belonged to Alan de Chepe, potter, and the eastern to John de Hadham, potter. When Alan died in 1311–12 he left his property to John de Hadham.

John de Hadham granted both properties to John son of Hugh Skynnere, whose executors in 1346 sold them together to Augustine le Waleys of Uxbridge and Robert atte Brome, rector of Henley. By 1363 both properties were held by Robert Gylle, upholder (probably a furniture dealer). He divided the western property so that from this date there were three separate units.

The westernmost property, next to Lord Zouche's, passed in the later fourteenth and fifteenth centuries through the hands of several poulterers. At this period only poulterers from outside the city were allowed to sell in Leadenhall; citizens could only sell from their shops and other accustomed places. Possibly these citizen poulterers, therefore, were setting up shop near to but not inside the public market, to take advantage of the crowds drawn to it, as well as of the opportunity to buy poultry in the market, in the last hour before it closed, for resale elsewhere. The fifteenth-century descent of the property is uncertain, but by 1484 it was held by William Heyborne the younger, and in 1514 was occupied by Anne Heyborne, widow.

More is known of the size and buildings on the middle of the three properties. It consisted of a plot just over 31 ft. (9.45 m.) wide along the street and 40 ft. (12.19 m.) deep, with a house or houses built within the plot, a

Trades in Early Modern London

The trades of shoemaker, cabinet-maker, and apothecary were practised in Lime Street and Leadenhall Street in the seventeenth century; elsewhere in London leatherworking, clothworking, and hatmaking were important.

(Above) A Cistercian monk *c.* 1500. St. Mary Graces had only ten monks besides the abbot at its dissolution in 1538.
(Below) Arms of the Vintners' Company, from a print of 1667.

vacant piece of ground enclosed with a stone wall, and a pond or well from which an outlet ran through a gutter into the street. There were three shops along the street frontage, with a gateway between the second and third to the house(s) at the back, and rooms over the shops and the gate. At least one of the shops was occupied by another poulterer.

The main house behind the shops was granted to William Pakenho, girdler, in 1373. He was dead by 1376, and his widow Edith lived there briefly, before granting it to Thomas de Matching of Essex. In 1380 he granted it to Henry Willingham or Bailly of Lessness in Kent. In 1399 and in 1412 it was held by Joan, widow of John Hare, stockfishmonger. The next known holder was John Thorp, chandler, who died in 1421. In 1437 the property was granted by William Sonyng, butcher, to Elias Davy and Thomas Bataill, mercers, and John Derby, draper, but its history after this date is unclear. In 1460 it was referred to as the dwelling-house (*mansio*) of William Feld, brewer.

The easternmost of the three properties held by Robert Gylle may have been the one he lived in. He died in 1385, and the next owner, William Frith, stockfishmonger, in 1386. It is not clear what happened next, but at some time the property passed to the new Cistercian abbey of St. Mary Graces by the Tower of London. The abbey was founded by Edward III in 1350, an act of piety probably inspired by the Black Death, and as well as extensive lands in East Smithfield outside the city it rapidly acquired many properties within the city from which it drew a large rent income. By 1392 the abbey had £3 6s. 8d. rent from property in Lime Street ward.

By 1535 the abbey's net income from all its properties in London and elsewhere was £547, which made it one of the richest Cistercian houses (only exceeded by Fountains and Furness), and one of the richest monasteries in or near London. It was dissolved by Henry VIII in 1538–9, and its estates passed to the Crown. In 1544 the abbey's former property in this parish, of which Richard Wadde was tenant, was sold to Hugh Losse. Losse was one of several great dealers in land at this time, able to take advantage of court connections to buy up some of the monastic estates the Crown had for sale. He and others like him bought up many London properties from the Crown, with the aim of reselling them quickly to those, often Londoners, who were looking for a specific property or location. It is likely that Losse sold this property soon, but its immediate purchaser is not known.

Pembridge's Inn

In 1313 the property on the corner of Leadenhall Street and Lime Street was held by Edmund de Bavent. Subsequently it passed to John Waleweyn, clerk, and from him to John de Hadham, the potter, to William of Shropshire (*de Salop*), glover, and in 1333 to Augustine le Waleys. It passed on his death to his widow Maud, and on her death in 1355 to their daughters Margaret, wife of William Carleton, and Margery, wife of John Maleweyn. The property was then worth £3 11s. a year.

In 1359 Sir John de Ludwyk, kt., and his wife Margaret, who may be Margaret Carleton, sold the whole property to Thomas de Lillingston of London. He died in 1361 and his widow and executors sold it later that year to Bernard Deos de Primerole, a Gascon vintner, probably from the Bordeaux region, but by this date a citizen of London by naturalisation. The Gascon wine trade, although much damaged by the Hundred Years War and plague and depopulation in the wine-growing regions, was still a very important feature of the London economy. Bernard may briefly have occupied this property, but he died early in 1362 and the King claimed his estates. He granted this to Sir Richard de Pembridge, to whom several London vintners subsequently released all claim in Bernard's lands.

(Above) Arms of the Merchant Taylors' Company, 1667.
(Below) Medieval building workers. Stone buildings survived in the city, sometimes for hundreds of years, but the timber-framed and plastered houses which predominated needed constant maintenance and repair.

Sir Richard evidently made this his London home, and it took its name of Pembridge's Inn from him. He died in 1375, as did his young son Henry: the heirs were Richard's nephews Sir Richard de Burley, kt., and Sir Thomas Barre, kt. Later in 1375 the property was partitioned, the northern half going to de Burley and the southern to Barre. The partition agreement mentions several houses, a hall, chambers, a close, a well, and a garden. Subsequently, however, Richard de Burley obtained the whole property, either buying out or inheriting Barre's share. He died in 1387. In 1399 the property was held by 'Lady de Ros', which probably means Beatrice, widow of Richard de Burley, whose first husband had been Thomas, Lord Ros, who had died in 1384.

In the early fifteenth century the property belonged to Thomas Sutton and William Holgrave, tailors. In 1428 they granted it to Ralph Holland, Richard Norden, Roger Holbech, and several other tailors. These grants probably concealed a trust on behalf of the Merchant Taylors' fraternity, which was fulfilled by the will of Ralph Holland in 1452 when he left the inn or messuage called 'Penbrigge Inne' on the corner of Lime Street to the Fraternity of Tailors and Linen Armourers of St. John the Baptist, the rents to be used to relieve poor members of the fraternity.

The early rent accounts of the Merchant Taylors' Company (as the fraternity became) in the 1450s and 1460s indicate that Pembridge's Inn was no longer a grand residence but had been divided up into numerous small units. There are references to the great hall, the great cellar, a storehouse, chambers over the gate, and other chambers and tenements, all in separate tenancies. The tenants seem to have been small craftsmen – a mattress-maker, a tailor, a mason, three carpenters, a sawyer, a spurrier, a painter, and a stainer – with also a chaplain, a waterman, and a fruiterer. Not all the rooms or tenements were occupied, so that of the total rent of over £26 due from all the parts of the property, only about £20–£22 was received in any year. Against this total must be set the cost of repairs to the houses, a constant drain of small sums – tiling, plastering, repairing hinges and catches – with occasional major structural works.

The Company's rent accounts for the later fifteenth and early sixteenth centuries were damaged or lost, so it is not possible to trace the tenants through that period. In 1545 the whole property (described as 'the tenement and timber house in Lymstrete and all the other tenements extending up to Ledenhall Strete') was held on lease from the Company by Stephen Kyrton, at £13 6s. 8d. rent; he was responsible for repairs. Kyrton was a leading member of the Company, master in 1542–3.

When in 1548 all chantries and 'superstitious' endowments were suppressed, the Merchant Taylors' Company, like many others, was faced with a serious problem. Many of its lands, though not in fact this property, had been given to it on condition that chantries or anniversary masses were maintained from the profits. The Crown was now claiming either these lands, or the annual amount formerly spent on maintaining these 'superstitious uses'. The Company decided that it must raise money to redeem these lands and charges from the Crown, especially since they included the land on which the Company's hall was built, and did so by selling off some of its unencumbered lands. Pembridge's Inn, with 'all houses, buildings, structures, chambers, garden, curtilages, and void plots' was accordingly sold to Stephen Kyrton in 1550.

Robert de Algate's property in Lime Street

In 1332 Robert de Algate granted the southern part, opening onto Lime Street, of his large property to Gilbert de Wigton, clerk. The land granted contained several houses, a garden, and two shops, and stretched from the garden of Leadenhall to the west to Lime Street to the east, and from the rest of Robert's property to the north to a garden called *le Posternhawe* to the south. *Le Posternhawe* probably took its name from the back gateway or postern from Leadenhall into Lime Street.

Gilbert de Wigton granted the same property in 1345 to Nicholas Podelcot of Abingdon, otherwise known as Nicholas de Abingdon. Nicholas died between 1361 and 1365. In 1386, after passing through the hands of a number of London citizens, probably none of whom lived there, the property was acquired by Sir Philip Sarnefeld, kt. He lived in part of the property, described as tenements, houses, and gardens, and there was a chapel attached to his house, suggesting an establishment of some status. In the rest of the property, however, there were small houses, shops, and gardens, one with an earth wall or bank, not a common feature in densely-occupied urban areas. Most of the occupants of these houses are not known, but John Plot, maltmonger, was one.

In the fifteenth century the property remained with noble or gentle families, and was held from 1427 to 1445 by Alice, countess of Oxford. By about 1450 it belonged to Thomas Broun. Broun, subsequently knighted, was a supporter of Henry VI during the conflicts of the 1450s. On Edward IV's victory and accession in 1461, therefore, he was attainted and his lands forfeited; in 1461 the new king granted them (including six houses and a garden in Lime Street) to Sir Thomas Vaughan, kt. Subsequently, but possibly not till after the Lancastrian/Tudor return in 1485, the Broun family regained the lands. In 1539 Sir Matthew Broun, kt., granted the property – now

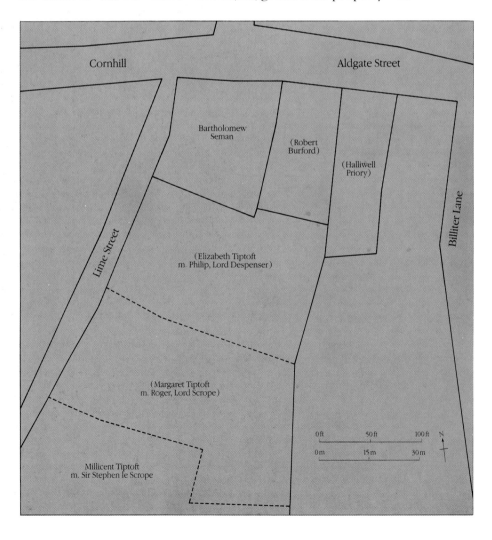

Plan of the properties east of Lime Street *c.* 1400 (see pp. 38–41).

described as a dwelling-house with seven shops and a garden – to Nicholas Leveson, citizen and Mercer and merchant of the Calais Staple. The property remained with the Leveson family till the later sixteenth century.

The Properties: East of Lime Street

The pattern of landholding on the east side of Lime Street was similar to that on the west in the medieval period, with properties along the frontage to Leadenhall Street (usually called Aldgate Street at this point until the sixteenth century) belonging to citizens, including several metalworkers, and larger properties behind belonging to noble or knightly families.

The earliest landowners known here are the abbey of Ramsey and the priory of Holy Trinity within Aldgate, in the early or middle twelfth century. Among their tenants by the late twelfth century were Henry le Feite and Richard Cavel, John Hornpit and Juliana his wife, and Gilbert son of Fulk or

Brass from St. Andrew Undershaft to Nicholas Leveson, mercer, sometime Sheriff of London, and merchant of the Calais Staple (*d*. 1539) and his wife Denys (*d*. 1560).

Fulcred of Lime Street. Another important landholder of the period was Theobald son of Ivo, an alderman, who had a stone house in Lime Street, and further east an orchard. Richard Cavel's house, at the upper end of the street, was also of stone, and in the sixteenth century the foundations of what must have been a twelfth-century stone house were excavated in Leadenhall Street. Stone houses were not uncommon in twelfth-century London, but were sufficiently unusual to be remarked on: they would have stood out among the wood, lath, and daub houses around them, and their occupants would have been important people.

Theobald's house lay close to the southern boundary of the parish and of Aldgate ward, under or to the south of the Lloyd's building of the 1950s. In the early thirteenth century, when he was about to go to Jerusalem on pilgrimage, Gilbert son of Fulk granted his house in Lime Street to the canons of Holy Trinity Priory within Aldgate. He does not seem to have returned, and in 1247–8 the canons granted the property, said to include a chapel, to Master William de Kilkenny, probably a cleric. William left the tenement to his nephew Richard son of Robert, who granted it to Philip Lovel in about 1257. It is not certain exactly where this property was but it too may have been on the Lloyd's site.

By the late thirteenth century there were three properties along Leadenhall Street and one very large one in Lime Street in the parish of St. Andrew Undershaft. The building in Lime Street which Lloyd's has occupied since the 1950s lies in part of the fourth of these.

The street-front properties

The corner property was held in 1291 by Gilbert de la Marche, potter. In 1350 it consisted of a brewhouse with ten shops and a garden, and in 1540 of six tenements, six gardens and several shops. The middle property, which in 1291 contained two houses and a garden or plot with trees growing, was by 1386 a brewhouse and garden, known by the name of the Pot on the Hoop, perhaps in allusion to the trade of its owner, Robert Ridere, potter or 'brasier'. Between 1392 and 1405 it belonged to Robert Burford, brasier or 'bellyettare'. By the mid sixteenth century all the houses on the property had disappeared and it was an open space.

The easternmost of the three properties belonged to Halliwell Priory, a nunnery in Shoreditch for Augustinian canonesses. Few of the priory's records survive, so most of the tenants are not known. The priory was dissolved in 1538, and in 1544 this property, described as a brewhouse with two adjacent gardens, was sold to Cyriac Pettyte of Canterbury.

The Tiptoft property

Behind the three street-front properties, and stretching south to the parish and ward boundary and beyond, was a single large property. In 1291 it belonged to the earl of Gloucester, Gilbert fitz Richard de Clare (d. 1295), one of the great magnates of Edward I's reign, who married Joan of Acre, Edward's daughter. It may have passed to his son and heir Gilbert fitz Gilbert, who was killed at Bannockburn in 1314, but it is not listed among the extensive estates the latter held at his death, and which were divided up between his three sisters. The descent of this property in the first half of the fourteenth century is therefore not clear.

By 1350 it belonged to Sir John Tybetot or Tiptoft, kt. He died in 1367, leaving a tenement in Lime Street to his son Robert. Robert Tiptoft died in 1372, leaving three young daughters. As was customary when a great landholder died leaving only daughters, the estate was divided equally between them. Sometimes this meant assigning separate properties to each, but in this case the one London property was partitioned. The northern part of the property went to Elizabeth, the youngest, the middle part to Margaret, the eldest, and the southern part ot Millicent, the second daughter.

Elizabeth Tiptoft's share

Elizabeth married Philip, Lord Despenser, and died in 1424 leaving one daughter, Margery. Margery married, as her second husband, Roger

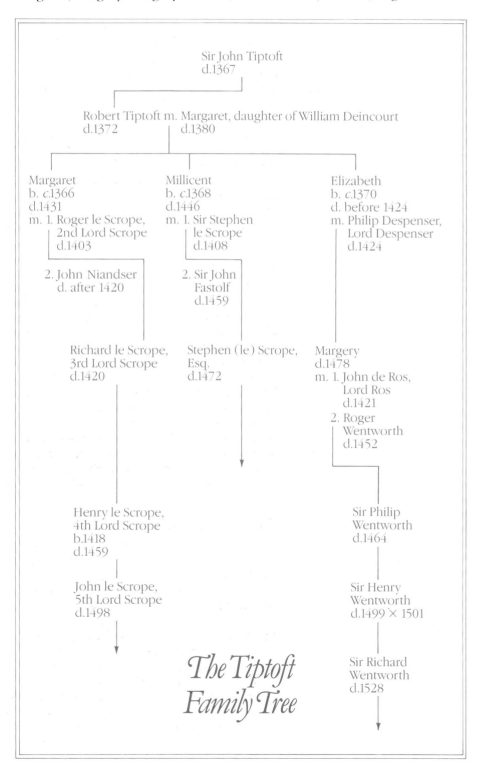

Sir John Tiptoft
d.1367

Robert Tiptoft m. Margaret, daughter of William Deincourt
d.1372   d.1380

Margaret
b. c.1366
d.1431
m. 1. Roger le Scrope,
2nd Lord Scrope
d.1403

2. John Niandser
d. after 1420

Millicent
b. c.1368
d.1446
m. 1. Sir Stephen
le Scrope
d.1408

2. Sir John
Fastolf
d.1459

Elizabeth
b. c.1370
d. before 1424
m. Philip Despenser,
Lord Despenser
d.1424

Richard le Scrope,
3rd Lord Scrope
d.1420

Stephen (le) Scrope,
Esq.
d.1472

Margery
d.1478
m. 1. John de Ros,
Lord Ros
d.1421

2. Roger
Wentworth
d.1452

Henry le Scrope,
4th Lord Scrope
b.1418
d.1459

Sir Philip
Wentworth
d.1464

John le Scrope,
5th Lord Scrope
d.1498

Sir Henry
Wentworth
d.1499 × 1501

The Tiptoft Family Tree

Sir Richard
Wentworth
d.1528

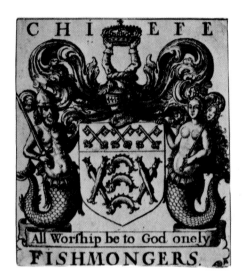

(Above) Arms of the Fishmongers' Company, 1667. *(Below)* Plan of Aldgate ward, early eighteenth century; north is to the left.

Wentworth (d. 1452), by whom she had a son Philip. Sir Philip Wentworth was involved in the Wars of the Roses on the Lancastrian side, and was captured and beheaded by the Yorkists after the battle of Hexham in 1464. His son (Sir) Henry, therefore, inherited on Margery's death in 1478, and died around 1500.

In 1508 Sir Richard Wentworth, son of Henry, granted all his lands in Lime Street 'which were the third part of Tiptot's lands' to John Nichylls, Merchant Taylor. Nichylls died in 1531, leaving the property, described as one capital messuage and garden, formerly three houses, one cottage, and two gardens, to his daughter Joan, wife of Thomas Offley. Offley later acquired the adjacent corner property on Lime Street and Leadenhall Street.

The 1950s Lloyd's building and the yard to the north of it must lie in part on the site of this property and in part on the site of the following one.

Margaret Tiptoft's share

Margaret Tiptoft inherited the central part of the property, which probably included the mansion house. She married Roger le Scrope, second Lord Scrope (d. 1403), and had a son Richard, third Lord Scrope, who fought at Agincourt (1415) and died in France in 1420. Margaret died in 1431 and the property passed to her grandson Henry, Lord Scrope of Bolton, who died in 1459. His heir was his son John, fifth Lord Scrope, who supported the Yorkist cause in the Wars of the Roses, subsequently welcomed Henry VII, made the mistake of supporting Lambert Simnel, was pardoned in 1488, and died in 1498. Either before or shortly after his death his property in Lime Street was sold to Richard Knight.

In 1501 Knight bequeathed the property to the Fishmongers' Company. At this time it was described as a great house with a garden and parlour, a tenter-yard (a place for stretching out fulled cloth), and six tenements. The 'great house' could represent the one once occupied by Sir John Tiptoft, and suggests that it had remained a grand residence and the town house of the Scropes. For the later history of this property see pp.144–6.

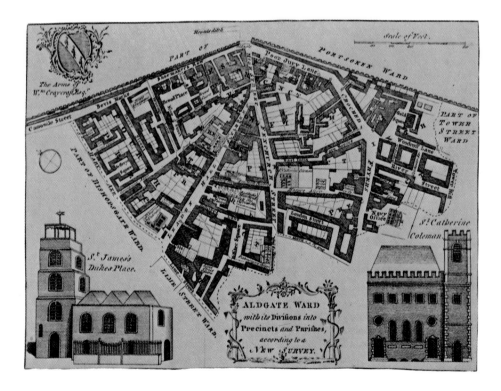

Millicent Tiptoft's share

Millicent, the second Tiptoft daughter, inherited the southern part of the property. She married Sir Stephen le Scrope, lord deputy of Ireland, and died in 1446. In 1452 Stephen Scrope, esquire, her son and heir, sold his property in Lime Street to Edmund Wydewell and John Harneys. It had previously been occupied by John Smith, carpenter, and was now in lease to John Wareham, carpenter.

In 1454 Wydewell and Harneys sold it to Thomas Wareham and others. It was described as two tofts of land (the sites of former houses) and two gardens, through which the common *fossa* or ditch of the city ran. This would have been one of the many open drainage channels or watercourses which networked the city. By his will dated 1477 and proved in 1482, Thomas Wareham, carpenter, left his dwelling-house, timber-yard (*le Tymberhawe*), and four gardens in Lime Street to the Carpenters' Company. The Company was to commemorate the anniversary of his death with masses in the churches of St. Dionis Backchurch and St. Andrew Undershaft.

The Carpenters' Company continued to hold the property, redeeming the chantry charge, or cost of observing Wareham's anniversary, from the Crown after 1548. The charge was then estimated at 8s. yearly. By the early seventeenth century, and probably earlier, the gardens had been partly built over, and several lettable properties created, with warehouses and yards. The occupants included several English and Dutch merchants. There was still a garden behind the houses and warehouses in 1731, with a mulberry tree growing in it.

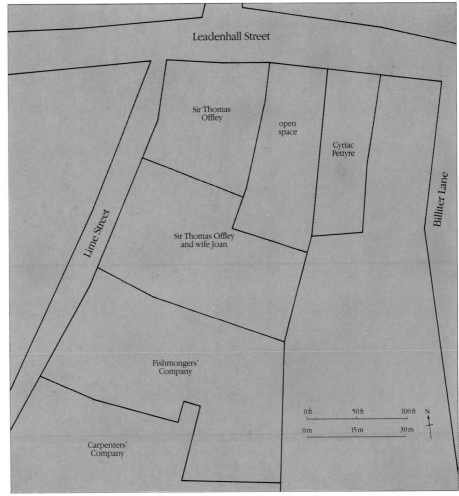

(Right) Plan of the properties east of Lime Street, *c.* 1560.
(Below) Stephen Scrope's deed of 1454, renouncing any right to the two tofts and gardens held by Thomas Wareham and others.

Chapter Three
Lime Street
before
Lloyd's

'London, capital of the most fruitful realm of England'. This engraving, published in 1572, derives from the 'Copperplate Map' of 1553–9 (p. 8), and shows London and Westminster on the eve of a period of rapid expansion.

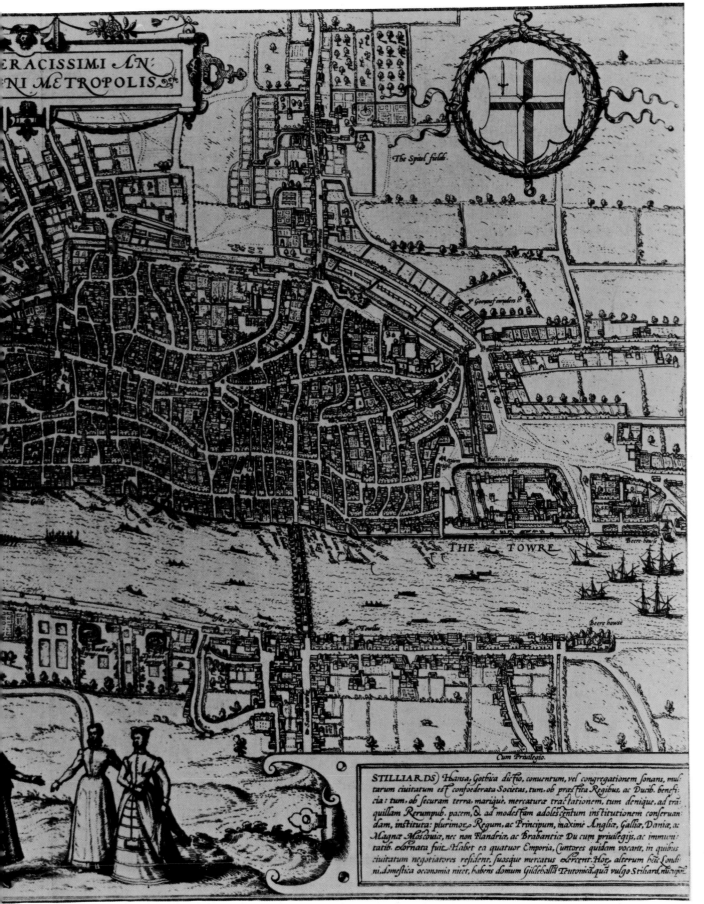

ERACISSIMI AN
NI METROPOLIS

The Spittel fieldt

S Georges croders &

Posterne Gate

THE TOWRE

Beere howse

Towrle   Beere howse

Cum Priuilegio.

STILLIARDS) Hansa, Gothica dictio, conuentum, vel congregationem sonans, mul-
tarum ciuitatum est confoederata Societas, tum ob praesita Regibus, ac Ducib. benefi-
cia: tum, ob securam terra, marique, mercaturae tractationem, tum denique, ad tra-
quillam Rerumpub. pacem, & ad modestam adolescentum institutionem conseruan-
dam, instituta: plurimor. Regum, ac Principum, maxime Angliae, Galliae, Daniae, ac
Magnae Moscouiae, nec non Flandriae, ac Brabantiae Ducum priuilegijs, ac immuni-
tatib. exornata fuit. Habet ea quatuor Emporia, Cuntores quidam vocant, in quibus
ciuitatum negotiatores resident, suasque mercatus exercent. Hor. alterum hîc Londi-
ni, domestica oeconomia nitet, habens domum Gildeballa Teutonica, qua vulgo Stiliard, nuncupant.

43

Chapter Three
Lime Street
before
Lloyd's II

The first Royal Exchange, founded by Sir Thomas Gresham in 1566, became an important place for merchants to meet and deal.

The sixteenth century saw many significant changes in London. For the first time since the fourteenth century there was sustained population growth, at first mostly accommodated in the expanding suburbs but later by increasing density of building and occupation in the centre. By 1600 the population of London, including Westminster, had perhaps reached 200,000. It was in the sixteenth century that London captured over 80% of the country's export and import trade, and really became a world city, a rival to Antwerp and a national and international marketplace. The Tudor monarchs' courts, though peripatetic, were often in or near London, and this and the presence of Parliament and the Law Courts made London the centre to which people were drawn on all kinds of business, and for fashionable pleasure.

The city of London in the sixteenth century was still ruled by its aldermen, and these were still for the most part merchants, often investors in the new chartered companies. The aldermen belonged to not more than ten or twelve of the city's hundred or more Livery Companies, principally the Mercers, the Grocers, the Drapers, the Haberdashers, the Clothworkers, and the Merchant Taylors. Although most of these Companies were nominally concerned with cloth production and trade, and in fact most of the leading members would have been involved in exporting cloth, by this time Company membership no longer necessarily reflected actual occupation or business concern. Any citizen, a member of any Company, might practise any

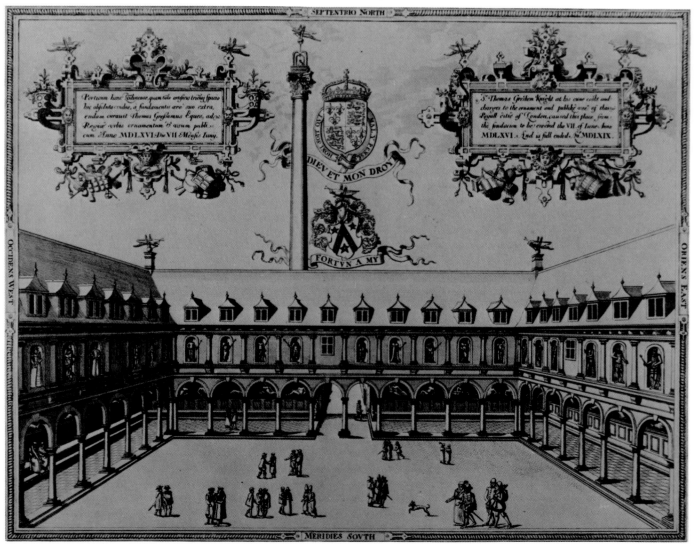

(Above) Arms and crests of Offley *(left)* and Woodroffe.
(Below) Simplified family tree showing the relationships between some of the owners of properties in the Lime Street area in the sixteenth century.

trade. Consequently the description 'citizen and Mercer' or 'Haberdasher', though it helps to identify individuals, no longer tells us much about them. The example of Thomas Rich, citizen and Mercer, 'by profession penman and schoolmaster' (p.64) makes this clear. There certainly were artisans and craftsmen in the Companies practising the trade indicated by the name, but it is only the small tradesmen, including non-citizens, who called themselves 'tailor', 'shoemaker', 'bookbinder', etc., whose occupations are certain.

The families of sixteenth- and seventeenth-century aldermen were often linked by blood and marriage, forming a complex kinship network through which wealth, and influence, could spread, and which may have been helpful to its members in business and city life. There were several such clusters of related families in the city, and the aldermanic families who owned property in the Lime Street area clearly formed one. Their wills show how important this network was: cousins, brothers- and sisters-in-law, children of a spouse's previous marriage, even the parents of a child's spouse, might be remembered. One example of the personal meaning of these ties is the way in which the unusual Christian name Grisel, borne by Nicholas Woodroffe's wife, whom John Stow the antiquarian commended in his account of this area, occurs again in succeeding generations among her relations and descendants. At the same time, however, individual families of high city rank were short-lived. Many aldermen and leading citizens were only first- or

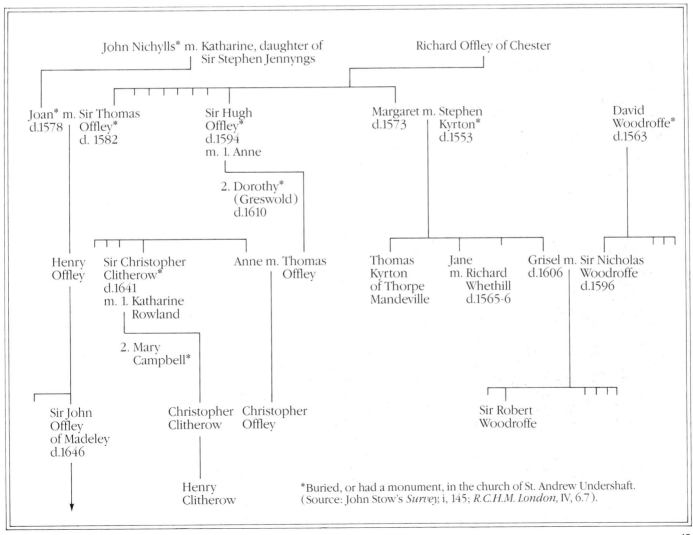

*Buried, or had a monument, in the church of St. Andrew Undershaft.
(Source: John Stow's *Survey*, i, 145; *R.C.H.M. London,* IV, 6.7).

second-generation Londoners, and their children or grandchildren, if the line lasted, were likely to be settled in the country, not necessarily in the area from which their ancestors came; the Offleys are a case in point.

One important change, in relation to the history of property, in early modern London, was in the way in which land was held and occupied. It became common for it to be let on leases of at least 21 years, at a relatively low rent but for a large initial payment, called a fine or income. The leaseholder was almost invariably responsible for keeping the property in repair and rebuilding when necessary. The leaseholder often sublet the property, sometimes to several tenants, at a much higher rent but usually without a fine or the security of a long lease, or liability for repairs. One effect of this was to transfer a much greater interest in the property to the leaseholder, and in a sense it is the market in leaseholds which in the seventeenth and eighteenth centuries really reflects changes in city life. Freeholds were still valued, for the income they brought and as a mortgageable security, but they are often found to be held by individuals residing outside London, perhaps the descendants of Londoners. Institutional property-holders, represented in this area by the East India Company, the Carpenters' and Fishmongers' Companies, Christ's Hospital and the parish of St. Andrew Undershaft, formed a significant proportion of city landlords.

In the early sixteenth century the pattern of properties to the west of Lime Street was still recognisably the same as in the medieval period. By the end of the century, some of the properties had been divided and recombined in several different ways, and it is not always possible to be sure

(Above) Arms of Clitherow, Kyrton, and Nichylls. *(Below)* Detail from the 'Copperplate Map' of 1553–9, with Lime Street in the centre. The streets were lined with houses, but behind them were yards and gardens, apparently laid out with beds and paths.

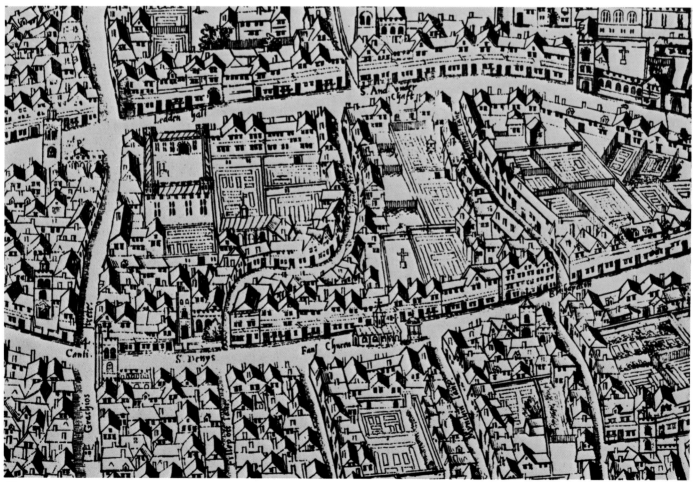

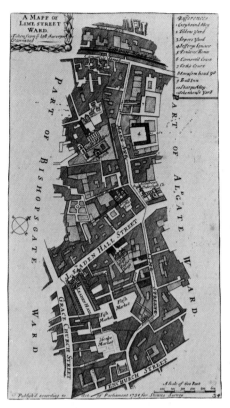

Lime Street ward in the eighteenth century. Leadenhall Market and East India House are clearly seen.

how the new pattern relates to the old. Clearly, however, the area was in the sixteenth and seventeenth centuries a 'good address', as the numbers of aldermen and even mayors who lived here indicates. The description of Sir Robert Lee's house (p.57) shows what style some of them could afford. Lee was perhaps exceptionally wealthy: in his will he left more than £1000 to each of his six children. It was typical of the city at this period that such large houses were interspersed with much smaller ones in which those providing services lived. The larger houses tended to be set back from the street, behind street-front houses and a yard, and several had gardens laid out for pleasure and recreation.

One reflection of the mercantile wealth of this area is the rebuilding of the parish church of St. Andrew Undershaft between 1520 and 1532. Stow says this was largely at the expense of Sir Stephen Jennings, Merchant Taylor (d. 1523), who was Mayor in 1508–9. Another benefactor was Nicholas Leveson of Lime Street; he and other contributors to the rebuilding were commemorated by armorial glass in the windows, and individually by their funeral monuments. The rebuilding was thorough: only the base of the tower remained from the old church. The plan is simple, and remarkably unconstricted for a city site. It has a nave, two aisles, and an almost flat ceiling; there is no chancel arch, though there would have been a rood-screen. The tower was repaired in the early eighteenth century, when there seems to have been extensive refurbishment of the church, and the upper part was rebuilt, with pinnacles, in 1883.

The internal arrangements of the church have been changed several times since it was built, following fashion and changes in liturgical practice. The monuments to sixteenth- and seventeenth-century parishioners are of particular interest, and include a brass to Nicholas Leveson (d. 1539), and monuments to Sir Thomas Offley (d. 1582), Dorothy widow of Sir Hugh Offley (d. 1610), Sir Christopher Clitherow (d. 1642), and Sir Anthony Abdy (d. 1640). The wall-monument to the antiquary John Stow (d. 1605), probably the parish's most famous inhabitant, is in the north aisle; the quill pen in his hand is renewed regularly.

That the church of St. Andrew Undershaft survives today is due to a freak of fortune, or the weather, in September 1666. The Great Fire began not far away in Pudding Lane, but most of its spread, thanks to the wind, was to the north-west and west. It burned St. Dionis Backchurch, at the south end of Lime Street, on the second day, and reached Leadenhall, but was checked there, perhaps partly by the high stone walls and open courtyard. The gardens and open ground in this quarter probably also inhibited it. Richard Briggenshaw, at the south end of the Lloyd's site to the west of Lime Street (p.69), lost one or more houses in the Fire; he was rebuilding in 1669.

Because this area largely escaped the Fire, sixteenth- and early seventeenth-century buildings survived here into the eighteenth and nineteenth centuries, to be drawn or engraved by topographical artists of that time. None now survives, however, and the best understanding of what such houses were like inside derives from the detailed descriptions of rooms and fixtures which accompany leases from the late sixteenth century.

The Great Fire provided the government of the city with the opportunity to reorganise all the city food markets, including Leadenhall. The aim was to remove them from the streets where they had traditionally been held to newly-cleared sites nearby where special accommodation could be provided. Earlier in the seventeenth century there was a herb market in Gracechurch Street (vegetables and dairy produce), a 'white' market in Leadenhall Street (poultry and meat except for beef), and a meat market, including beef, in Leadenhall itself and the Greenyard. The white market was removed to the Greenyard, part of Leadenhall, in 1657. In addition, there were alternate markets for tanned leather and raw hides in Leadenhall, and

St.Andrew Undershaft

The church shown here and surviving today dates largely from the sixteenth century, but the tower was rebuilt in the nineteenth century. John Stow's monument *(bottom left)* is in the north aisle.

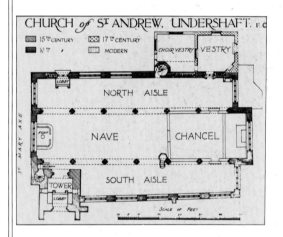

St. Andrew Undershaft Leadenhall Street.

the buildings were used to store grain, wool, and cloth (also sold there). The East India Company rented part of the building for warehousing from 1617.

After the Fire, three new market-places were laid out, with stalls and shops, incorporating part of the old building of Leadenhall. The herb market was brought in from the street, and the white and beef markets also accommodated. Woollen cloth continued to be sold there too, in the Woolhall and the Colchester and Suffolk Bay Halls, but in decreasing quantity over the years. The market was not extensively altered until 1879–80, when the buildings were demolished and the present market begun. Leadenhall market is now the only fresh produce retail market surviving within the city.

It was in the late sixteenth and seventeenth centuries that the practice of identifying houses by signs became common. House-signs existed in the Middle Ages, and many taverns had a sign or symbol hung outside, but the growing density and complexity of streets and houses in the sixteenth century meant that more tradesmen and ordinary householders now hung out distinguishing signs. Some were common all over the city – the Bell, the Mermaid, the Anchor, the Flower de Luce – but others like the Blackmore and Camel (p.56) may have been unique.

In the seventeenth and eighteenth centuries the development of the

Detail from a plan of the city in 1667, showing the extent of the Great Fire's destruction. The stone walls of Leadenhall and the open gardens and yards behind prevented the flames from reaching Leadenhall Street.

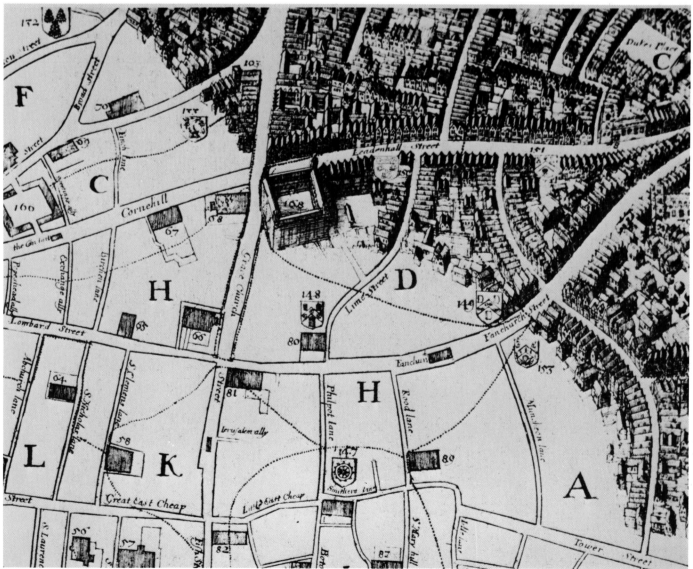

block to the west of Lime Street was governed by the expansion of the East India Company's premises. The Company, founded 1599–1600, came into the area in 1635, renting rooms in Sir Christopher Clitherow's house, and in 1648 moved a few doors away to rent Lord Craven's house. It also rented warehouses and other premises in Lime Street. It bought the freehold of Lord Craven's property in 1710, and further properties in the 1720s, before building its first classical street-front mansion on Leadenhall Street in 1726–9. More lands and houses were acquired in Lime Street in the 1750s and incorporated into the complex of yards and warehouses there behind the main house. The last remaining houses on Leadenhall Street to the east of East India House, up to the corner of Lime Street, and the houses in Lime Street, were acquired piecemeal in the 1790s, before the full-scale rebuilding of the whole site in 1796–9. The houses to the west of East India House, once known as the Green Gate but by then as Russia Court, were acquired by the Company and demolished for further buildings in the early nineteenth century.

It is noticeable how long small tradesmen persisted in Leadenhall and Lime Street. The East India Company's presence no doubt attracted merchants to the area, and stimulated the building of more warehouse

Detail from a plan of the rebuilt city in 1676, showing the new market-places at Leadenhall. 'B 88' denotes East India House, 'B 66' the church of St. Andrew Undershaft.

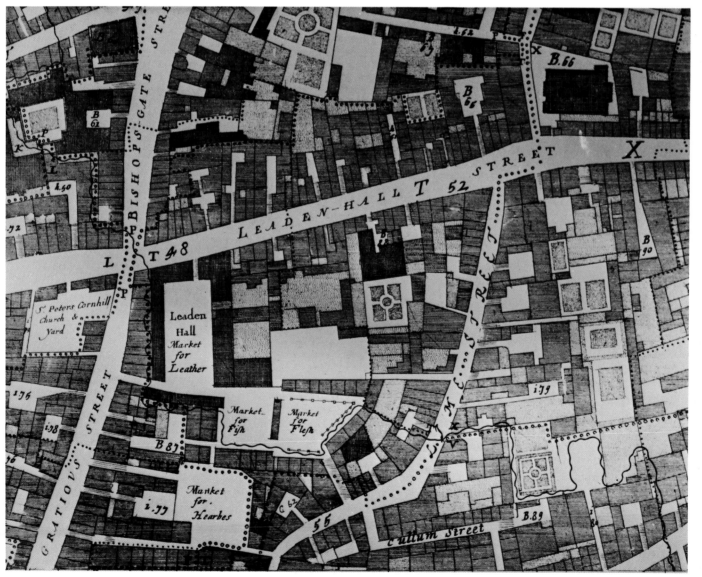

accommodation nearby, but of those properties not taken over by the Company until the 1790s (pp.59–65) several were still being used for unrelated trades, including those of trunk-maker and cabinet-maker, and one was a tavern.

It is the fact that this block was taken over by one large institution in the eighteenth century that makes it possible to tell so much of the story. The title deeds to most parts of the site were acquired and kept by the East India Company, and transferred to subsequent owners of the site; a few records remained at the India Office. The same detail is not available for the block east of Lime Street, but as much of it as can be known is told on pp.143–7.

The Properties: West of Lime Street

The following account gives the histories of each part of the site west of Lime Street, down to their acquisition and redevelopment by the East India Company. An architectural account of the successive buildings used by the Company is given in Chapter 6.

Leadenhall Street

Lime Street

Buildings
Gardens
Yards or open space
Approximate extent of the Great Fire

| 0 ft | 50 ft | 100 ft | N |
| 0 m | 15 m | 30 m | |

(Above) Arms of the Skinners' Company, 1667.
(Right) The Lime Street area in 1676, redrawn to a more accurate scale from the plan on p. 51. The bolder lines denote the boundaries of separate freehold properties.

The Green Gate

The Green Gate, held by John Meautis in 1507 and 1517, had returned to the Crown's hands by 1558, when Philip and Mary granted it via intermediaries to David Woodroffe, citizen and Haberdasher. He lived there until his death in 1563; his son Sir Nicholas Woodroffe, citizen and Haberdasher, later mayor, lived in the Green Gate with his wife Grisel until 1588. By this time Nicholas seems to have been running into financial difficulty: he resigned his aldermanry, normally held for life, in that year, and sold the Green Gate to John Moore, citizen and Skinner, later alderman. The four houses that went with it had been reduced to three, possibly by rebuilding. Moore, and after him his widow Mary, occupied the main house in the late sixteenth century.

Subsequently the Green Gate seems to have been reclaimed by the Crown. It was granted in 1615 to Sir Lewis Tresame, kt., Bt., a gentleman of the King's chamber, who granted it before 1617 to Levinus Munck, esquire, one of the clerks of the King's signet. In 1622 Munck sold the whole property to Katharine Manning of London, widow, and her son John Manning, for £2500. The main house was still known as the Green Gate, and the three others, occupied separately, were known as the Mermaid, the Flower de Luce (formerly the Anchor), and the Bell.

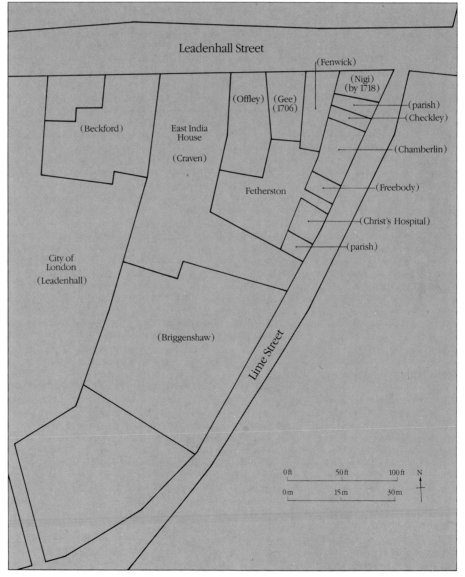

(Above) Arms of the Haberdashers' company, 1667.
(Right) Plan of the properties west of Lime Street, *c.* 1700.

Leadenhall Market

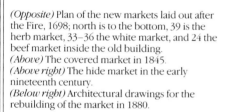

LEADEN HALL MARKET.

(Opposite) Plan of the new markets laid out after the Fire, 1698; north is to the bottom, 39 is the herb market, 33–36 the white market, and 24 the beef market inside the old building.
(Above) The covered market in 1845.
(Above right) The hide market in the early nineteenth century.
(Below right) Architectural drawings for the rebuilding of the market in 1880.

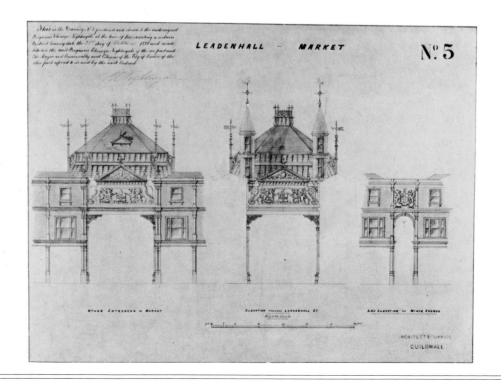

LEADENHALL - MARKET   Nº 5

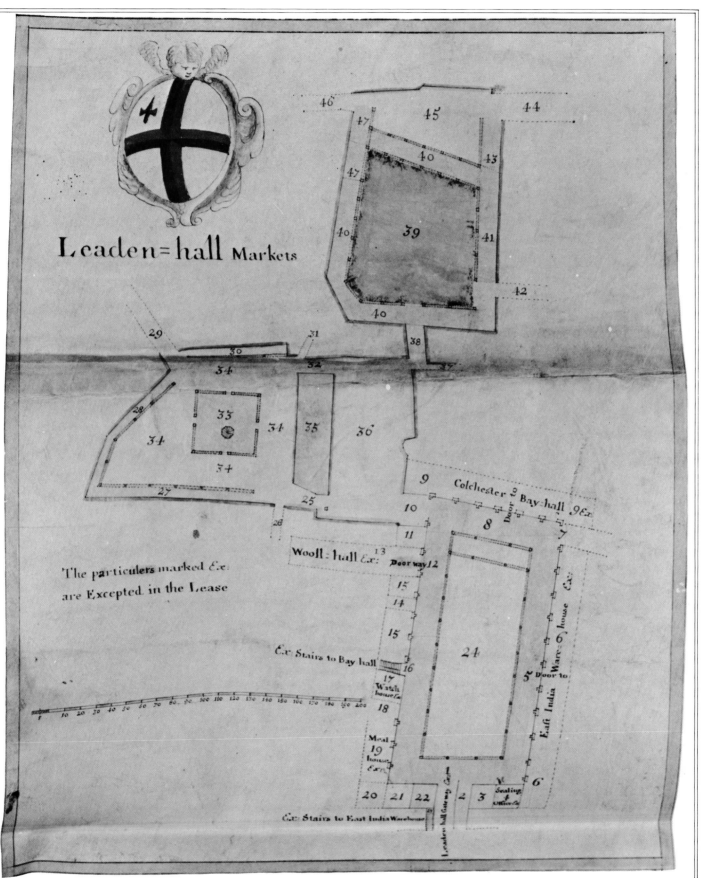

Leaden=hall Markets

The particulers marked Ex: are Excepted in the Lease

(Above) Arms of the Drapers' Company, 1667.
(Below) Three houses, part of the Green Gate,
built probably in the seventeenth century and
demolished shortly after 1800. One of them can
also be seen to the right of the larger illustration
on p. 59.

In 1632 the Green Gate was occupied by Lawrence Halsted, citizen and
Draper; a Mrs Whiting lived in the Flower de Luce, paying £18 rent, and
Christopher Wickens in the Bell, paying £20 rent. Katharine Manning and her
grandson John sold the freehold but kept a 99-year lease on the property; the
Mermaid may have been sold separately at this time. By 1684 the freehold
was held by Thomas Papillon, and the 99-year lease had passed on John
Manning's death to his sisters, and to their sons. In that year both freehold
and leasehold interests were transferred to Thomas Price, citizen and
Goldsmith, for a total of £3654. Thomas Canham, merchant, lived in the
Green Gate, and Matthew Gibbons and John Hall in the other two houses.
Price then leased the property to Sir Thomas Beckford for 1000 years at a
peppercorn rent.

Nineteenth-century engravings of East India house show a row of three
elaborately-decorated houses to the west of it. These must be part of the
Green Gate; possibly, like several other of the properties in this area, the
main house was set back behind street-front houses. The three houses
probably date from the seventeenth century, but the date of rebuilding is not
known.

In the later seventeenth and eighteenth centuries the property
descended in the Beckford family. In 1760 the Green Gate was occupied by
Samuel and Thomas Stratton and John Redbard, merchants, at £100 rent, and
the other two houses by Elizabeth Rice at £60, and Benjamin Forfit at £44. In
1783 Peter Beckford of Stepleton, Dorset, leased the property that had once
been the Green Gate but was now called Russia Court, with three houses or
tenements (this did not include the houses held by Rice and Forfit),
warehouses, cellars, etc., for £100 rent, to Samuel Stratton and his partner
Charles Pieschett, merchants. In 1800 the East India Company bought the
whole property. It was not incorporated into the 1796–9 rebuilding, and the
houses on the street survived until the 1800s, when they were pulled down.

The Bell and the Blackmore and Camel

Between the houses comprising the Green Gate on the west, and Sir William
Craven's house on the east, there were in the seventeenth century two small
separate freehold properties called the Bell (the western one) and the Rose,
afterwards the Blackmore and Camel (the eastern one). It is not clear what
medieval property or properties they represent. The Blackmore and Camel
was acquired by Lord Craven in 1636, the Bell probably by 1650 and certainly
by 1690. They were included in the sale of Lord Craven's lands to the East
India Company in 1710, but continued to be occupied by tenants until the
1720s. The sites of the two properties formed part of the site for the new East
India House built in 1726–9.

Craven House, later East India House

The great property once held by the Zouche family (see p.32) stretching
from Leadenhall Street down to Lime Street came into the Crown's hand on
the suppression of the chantries in 1548, and was sold to Thomas White and
Stephen Kyrton, aldermen. Kyrton also acquired Pembridge's Inn, but seems
to have occupied the main house on this site until his death in 1553. His
widow Margaret lived there until 1573. In 1575 it was leased to Stephen
Woodroffe, citizen and Haberdasher. In 1580 Thomas Starkey, alderman,
already living there, acquired the freehold from Thomas Kyrton of Thorpe
Mandeville, Northants., son of Stephen.

In the last years of the sixteenth century the property was acquired and
substantially rebuilt by (Sir) Robert Lee, citizen and Merchant Taylor. He
probably held his mayoral year (1602–3) here. After his death in 1605 it

(Above) Arms of the Mercers' Company, 1667.
(Right) Part of the inventory of fixtures attached to the lease of East India House in 1675. This section covers the contents of the porch, the great chamber, and the chambers over the kitchen and the hall and adjoining and under the leads.

passed to his son Robert, who in 1607 leased it to (Sir) William Craven, another Merchant Taylor, later Lord Mayor (1610–11), for 21 years at £8 rent and an initial fine or cash payment of £1200. The property was said to be 'in Cornehill Street' (Leadenhall Street), but with a back gate opening into Lime Street.

A detailed inventory of the house's fittings was drawn up to accompany the lease. This makes the size and style of the house clear, though not its precise layout. There was a small old building, included in the lease, on Leadenhall Street, but the main house was set back behind outer and inner gates and a yard. It was substantial, even palatial. There were the usual domestic offices of a large house (kitchen, larder, pastry, buttery, scullery, scouring-house, wash-house), a great hall, great parlour, great dining-chamber, and several chambers and a gallery upstairs. There were also counting-houses, warehouses, and cellars, and one room set up as a working room for a tailor. At the back were more yards, a stable, the garden, and the back gate to Lime Street.

The house was richly fitted. In the great hall there was a carved screen with Queen Elizabeth's arms, a frame for the Lord Mayor's sword of office, and cupboards 'all carved and garnished with imagerie'. There was a candle-frame, described as 'a fair gilt beam with five brass candlesticks and an angel over the same', suspended by iron chains. The great parlour was wainscoted (panelled), with an alabaster chimneypiece and over it the Queen's arms and pictures or carvings of St. George, Justice, and Charity. The great dining chamber was also panelled and had 'a mantletree very curiouslie carved and gilt with the story of the Creation'. Some of the chambers had marble hearths or painted tiles, as did the gallery. In the garden there was a paved walk, with carved posts and rails, and a banqueting-house, a sort of summer-house, with green and yellow tiles. Banqueting-houses were an important adjunct to gracious living, and several large city mansions are known to have had one. The Fishmongers' Company had one in its garden on the east side of Lime Street (pp.145–6).

Clearly Sir Robert Lee had lived in style, and this was a fitting house for a

Hearth Tax return for the parish of St. Andrew Undershaft in 1673. The list begins at the west end of the parish with the inhabitants of the Green Gate. The numbers represent hearths in each house.

leading city merchant such as Sir William Craven. He died in 1618, and the freehold was bought, probably in 1623, by his widow. Sir William's son, later Lord Craven, was a courtier rather than a city man, and certainly in the late seventeenth century his town house was in Drury Lane. In 1638 Thomas Atkins, one of the sheriffs that year, lived in the house, continuing the tradition of occupation by leading citizens. In 1648, however, the East India Company, until that date renting part of Sir Christopher Clitherow's house nearby (see p.61), took a lease of this house from Lord Craven.

This was the time of the English Civil War, followed by the Commonwealth and Protectorate. Lord Craven took no active part in the war, spending those years on the continent, but Parliament considered him to be a Royalist and in 1651 his lands were confiscated. The East India Company took a new lease from the Parliamentary Committee for Compounding, but in 1653 the trustees for the sale of forfeited lands sold 'all that capital messuage and appurtenances, partly brick and partly timber, in Leadenhall Street... commonly called East India House' to Edward Tooke, esquire, for £2785. It is interesting to note how quickly the name had become attached to the property, even though the Company had only a leasehold interest.

With the restoration of Charles II in 1660, all forfeited Royalist lands were restored. Lord Craven returned to England, and in 1661 leased both the main tenement in Leadenhall Street and the back one in Lime Street to the East India Company at £100 rent and £1000 fine or cash payment. The inventory accompanying this lease is similar to that of 1607, but with rather less detail. In 1673 East India House had 18 hearths, according to the Hearth Tax return.

The Company took a new lease of the premises from Lord Craven in 1675. The schedule to this lease lists the same rooms as before, with some of the same fittings, including the hanging candle-frame in the hall and the chimneypiece carved with stone figures in the parlour. But much more of the furniture is listed, mostly benches, tables, and chairs. The little parlour had a walnut table, green curtains, one elbow chair and two 'back chairs' covered in green. The great chamber, reached by stairs from the porch and probably overlooking the garden, seems to have been the principal court or committee room. It had a walnut table and also one topped with white marble, supported by four lions and five pillars; panelling; tapestry hangings; and a gilded chimneypiece. In one of the upper chambers next to the leads was 'one cracked picture of Adam and Eve', possibly the 'story of the Creation' that formed part of the decoration of the great dining chamber in 1607. There was a shuffle-board in the long gallery.

The East India Company remained tenants of Lord Craven, who died in 1697, and of his heirs, until 1710. Then, after some deliberation, they bought the freehold of the site (including the Blackmore and Camel, the Bell, and the Ship) for £4000. The settlement of some leasehold and mortgage claims took longer.

The Company had been modifying the back parts of the premises for some time, to suit their needs. They leased some ground out of Leadenhall from the Mayor and Corporation in 1683, and began building warehouses on this and on part of the garden of East India House in 1686. It was not until the 1720s, however, that they decided to rebuild the main house. By that time it must have been over 120 years old; some of it, if the front part had not been included in Robert Lee's rebuilding, older still. The story of the eighteenth-century rebuildings, and of the new style of accommodation they provided, is given in Chapter 6.

The Ship

The later-sixteenth-century owners and occupants of the house immediately to the east of the one that became East India House are not known. In 1614 it

(Above) 'East India House' in the late seventeenth century. This is clearly not the main house, which lay back from the street frontage, and could in fact be the next-door house which was known as the Ship.
(Below) The new East India House, after 1729.

belonged to Ursula Scarlet of Waltham and her son John. In contrast to Craven's house at this date it was a narrow upright one, with no yard of its own, and at least three floors and garrets. The hall and chamber, on the first floor, had bay windows the full width of each room, as did the chambers above them. By 1621 the house was occupied by John Ball, citizen and Ironmonger. Dame Elizabeth Craven, widow of Sir William, acquired a long leasehold by 1623, and sublet the house. In 1625 the Scarlet family sold the freehold, subject to the long leasehold, to the Turners' Company; the Turners sold it to Lord Craven in 1670.

It seems possible that the earliest pictures of 'East India House', in the late seventeenth century, actually show the Ship, owned like East India House by Lord Craven though not occupied by the Company. The name 'the Ship' first occurs in 1661, and it was in 1660–1 that the famous ship paintings on the facade of 'East India House' were made. The royal arms, and the arms of the East India Company, which do not occur on all versions of the engraving, may have been added later. The freehold of the Ship was sold with East India House to the Company in 1710.

Sir John Offley's property

This house lay next to the Ship, but did not come into the East India Company's possession until 1796. It is probably therefore the shop-front shown to the east of East India House in eighteenth-century engravings. For some reason very few records relating to this property survive.

In 1641 it belonged to Sir John Offley of Madeley, Staffs., who was descended from Sir Thomas Offley, one of a large family who had come to London in the sixteenth century and prospered there. It is likely that this property had belonged to Sir Thomas, who certainly lived in this parish at one time, though he may not have lived in this house. Sir John Offley

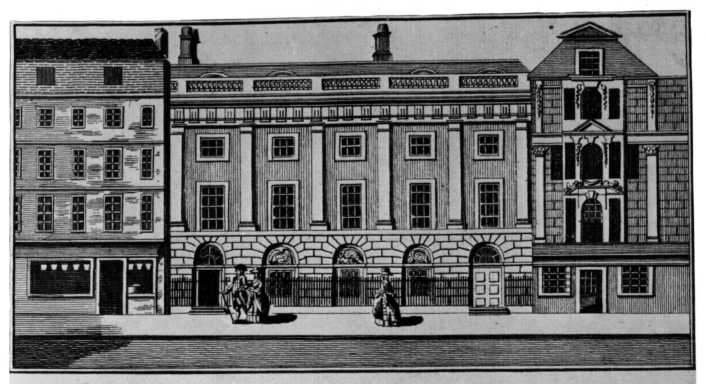

probably had no city business and certainly did not live in this house. He was the friend and patron of Izaak Walton, who dedicated 'The Compleat Angler' to him.

The property descended in the Offley family, and by 1704 was occupied by an apothecary, a cabinet-maker, and a cooper. In 1721 it was sold to William Withers of London, esquire. He left it to his son William Withers, who in 1765 settled it in an unbreakable trust on his daughter Elizabeth. She married John Goldsborough Ravenshaw in 1771. In 1796, when they were negotiating with the East India Company to sell the property, the Company's counsel thought that an Act of Parliament might be necessary to circumvent the settlement. In the event the property, occupied since at least 1765 by Joseph Swift, trunkmaker, at £60 rent, was sold to the Company for £2300.

Sir Christopher Clitherow's house

The early history of this property, the next east from Offley's, is not known, but it seems clear that it incorporated at the back some land that had formerly been part of Pembridge's Inn. It had access to Lime Street, which

Monument in the church of St. Andrew Undershaft to Sir Thomas Offley (*d.* 1582) and his wife Jane or Joan (*d.* 1578).

none of the medieval properties on the street front between Lord Zouche's house and Pembridge's Inn had had. The date at which this rearrangement was made is not known.

By 1625 the property was owned and occupied by Christopher Clitherow, M.P. for London 1628–9, Lord Mayor 1635–6, knighted 1636. Part of the premises, possibly the small house at the front, was occupied by a tenant, Francis Gilbert, clothworker. In 1635 Clitherow let part of his house to the merchants of the East India Company, who had quitted Crosby House in Bishopsgate because of the high rent demanded when their lease ran out. Clitherow was a member of the Company and its governor in 1638. The Company paid him £150 rent, reduced in 1643, after Sir Christopher's death in 1642, to £100, but they found the accommodation too cramped, with not enough warehousing, and from 1642 at least were looking for somewhere else to move to. After negotiations, it was decided in 1647 to take a lease of Lord Craven's house, which must have been much larger, from 1648.

After Sir Christopher's death the freehold passed to his son, Christopher, and by 1681 to the latter's son Henry Clitherow. The tenant then was Peter Devetts, merchant. A small part of the garden, cut off from the rest by a brick

(Above) Arms of Clitherow.
(Right) Monument in the church of St. Andrew Undershaft to Sir Christopher Clitherow (*d.* 1642) and his second wife Dame Mary Campbell (*d.* 1645).

wall, was leased by Clitherow to the tenant of the Ship, to use as a yard. By 1695 Henry Clitherow had divided his property in two, selling 'an old timber building', probably the front part, to Robert Master, and the greater part at the back to Sir Heneage Fetherston. The latter is described on p.67, below.

In 1706 the front part of the property was bought by Joshua Gee, citizen and Grocer, for £2330. It descended to his younger son Osgood Gee, and by 1736 was occupied as three tenements. It was substantially rebuilt in 1767 by one of the tenants, to whom all three leases had been assigned. In 1792, when the freehold belonged to Osgood Gee the younger, the leaseholder Catherine Sharp assigned all three leases to the East India Company. Osgood Gee sold the freehold in 1796.

In the assignment of 1792 the three houses were referred to as 'front house', 'back house', and 'Upholders' Hall'. The Upholders' Company had held the lease of one of the three houses since 1736, but there is very little evidence in their records of the use they made of it; certainly the court did not meet there, and since the property seems to have consisted mostly of warehouses perhaps 'Hall' is a misnomer.

The front house was four storeys high, and its fixtures included a water-

Detail from an eighteenth-century view of Leadenhall Street *(see p. 124),* showing the houses between East India House *(right)* and the top of Lime Street *(left)*

Arms and crest of Woodroffe.

tank on the roof and a 'fire-engine', probably a pump, on the leads, an iron bath and shower bath, and a system of bells. The back house was at least three storeys high, plus a garret, and was heated by several 'cast iron air stoves'. 'Upholder's Hall' had a yard and warehouses, a kitchen, and a counting-house with another stove. There was a 'forcing pump' for water in the yard, and iron gates to the street.

Sir Nicholas Woodroffe's house

This may represent the property held by the abbey of St. Mary Graces until the Reformation (see p.34). Richard Whethill, citizen and Merchant Taylor, had bought it by 1548, and appears to have sold it by 1552 to Stephen Kyrton, alderman, who already owned a great deal of property in this parish. He settled this property on his daughter Grisel and her husband (Sir) Nicholas Woodroffe, and they may have lived here at first before moving to the Green Gate.

After Nicholas Woodroffe's death in 1596, and Grisel's in 1606, this property passed to Sir Robert Woodroffe, their second son. After several family settlements and mortgages, by 1664 the property was held by John Woodroffe on a thousand-year lease. By this time it comprised two shops and a tavern called the Hoop Tavern. In 1681 both freehold and long leasehold were acquired by Edward Fenwick, who granted a long rebuilding lease to Robert Rossington. In 1683 the tavern, now called the Hoop and Griffin, was occupied by Griffith George, vintner, and the two shops on the street, one either side of the entrance, by a periwig-maker and an oilman.

Edward Fenwick the younger sold the freehold to Samuel Rush in 1724, and it descended in that family, while the leasehold was held by the descendants of Tanner Arnold, to whom Rossington had assigned it. In 1734 the Hoop and Griffin was leased to Katharine Wisdome. The tavern had carved doorposts and a deal-panelled passage from the street to the tavern, with stairs going down under the periwig-maker's shop to the cellars. There was a bar-room, and a large panelled room with 'boxes', as in a coffee-house, tables, and benches, and a tiled fireplace. There were more boxes and benches in the passage leading to the kitchen, and two yards, the front one paved in black marble and Purbeck squares. Upstairs were several panelled rooms, including one with 'beleccion work' and a black and white marble hearth.

In 1794 the East India Company bought the freehold of the property from William Beaumaris Rush, and the leasehold from Stephen Todd.

Pembridge's Inn

In 1550 Stephen Kyrton, master of the Merchant Taylors' Company, bought from them the property once known as Pembridge's Inn. It seems probable that he did not live in this property but in the one further west that later became East India House. He died in 1553, leaving all the properties he had bought from the Merchant Taylors to his wife Margaret for life. On her death the property descended to their son Thomas. In 1598, as Thomas Kyrton of Thorpe Mandeville, Northants., he sold it to William Morton of Thorpe Mandeville.

By this date the property consisted of about a dozen houses in Lime Street; the greater part of the property at the back had been transferred at an unknown date to the property on Leadenhall Street later held by Sir Christopher Clitherow. From 1601 onwards, William Morton, now of Croydon, Surrey, sold off the houses, singly or in parcels of two or three, mostly to the people already occupying them. It is thought that one of the houses was occupied by the antiquary and historian John Stow, but the deeds

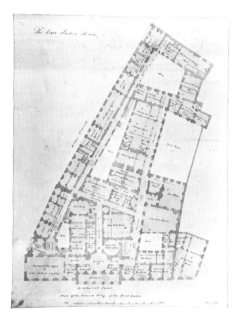

Ground-floor plan of the rebuilt and extended East India House, 1820.

do not make it possible to say which. Each therefore has a separate history from the early seventeenth century. These are given in order from the Leadenhall Street end, under the headings of the first known owners after Morton. It seems likely that most or all of the houses were identical in type, probably built as a row, narrowing from north to south, with rooms arranged as in Thomas Hedge's house (p.64). The access gate to Clitherow's property probably lay between two of the more southerly houses.

John Steward's properties

In 1607 William Morton sold the corner property on Leadenhall Street to John Steward, citizen and Pewterer. In 1638 it was occupied by a Mr Steward and valued at £26 per annum. John Steward, son of Roland Steward, sold it in 1657 to Edmund Lewin, citizen and Merchant Taylor, for £400. In 1718 Margaret Nigi, daughter of Edmund Lewin, left the property, now two houses, to her sons (possibly sons-in-law) John Hunt and the Revd. Joseph Wilcocks, D.D., chaplain to George I.

John Hunt assigned his house, known as the Swan and situated on the corner, to Wilcocks, by now bishop of Gloucester, in 1725. Joseph Wilcocks subsequently became bishop of Rochester, and died in 1756, leaving a considerable estate to his son Joseph, who became a noted antiquary. In 1787 the Swan was occupied by Mary Probert, widow, and the other house, to the west of the Swan in Leadenhall Street, by William Finer, cabinet-maker. The younger Joseph Wilcocks left the property to his cousins Rachel Wilks and John Lodge in 1792, and in 1795 they sold it to the East India Company.

John Le Roy's house

The first house from the corner of Leadenhall Street was sold by William Morton to its tenant, John Le Roy, 'ordinary post for France and free denizen of England', in 1603. In 1634 his widow Mary sold it to Thomas Rich, citizen and Mercer, for £168. In his will of 1672, Rich, 'by profession penman and schoolmaster' of West Ham, left this property, now occupied by Theophilus Davies, apothecary, to trustees of the parish of St. Andrew Undershaft. Out of the rent they were to pay for two annual sermons, thanking God for his mercy in preserving this and Rich's other properties, and the whole parish, from the 'late dreadful and devouring Fire' of 1666.

The parish trustees let the house to a succession of tenants including a surgeon, a blacksmith, and a vintner, but none of these leases includes details of the house. The East India Company offered to buy the house in 1795, and after deliberation the vestry agreed; the purchase price (not recorded) was invested to produce an income to maintain the trust.

Thomas Hedge's house

The next house south from John Le Roy's was sold by Morton to Thomas Hedge in or before 1607. At that time it was occupied by Richard Hedge, tailor. In 1665 Thomas Hedge of Adson, Northants., sold it to Edward Checkley, citizen and Merchant Taylor. It was called the Golden Heart and was occupied by Henry Wickliffe. Clearly it was a narrow row-house, comprising only a cellar, a ground-floor shop, a dining-room and kitchen on the first floor, two chambers on the second floor, two chambers on the third, and a garret above.

The freehold descended to Edward Checkley's son, to his widow Susanna, to her sister Hannah Wolford, and from her to John Scott in 1741. The tenant then was William Ridge. In 1749 John Scott left his property in Lime Street to his cousins. The last of these, Mary Smart, died in 1776, leaving this house to Ann Parker of Shoreditch. The tenant then and when Ann Parker sold the house to the East India Company in 1796 was Mr Holme.

Thomas Newe's house

In 1607 William Morton sold the third house from the corner to Thomas Newe, blacksmith. In 1634 Thomas Newe's son, also Thomas, sold it to Henry Sherman, blacksmith. It descended to Richard and Edward Sherman, blacksmiths, who in 1663 leased it to Thomas Darker, another blacksmith. In 1673 it was occupied by John Porter, and had two domestic hearths and one forge. The association with smithing did not persist much longer, however, and in 1677 the tenant was Nathaniel Hiller, bookbinder.

In 1677 the Shermans sold the house to John Chitwell, citizen and Carman, who in 1687 sold it to Joseph Chamberlin, citizen and Blacksmith (not necessarily a practising smith). Chamberlin also acquired the three houses to the south of this one. The freehold of the four houses descended in the Chamberlin family until 1740, when they passed, as the result of an earlier mortgage, to John Reynolds. By his will of 1749 he left them to his nephew John Vincent, who in 1783 left them to his son, also John Vincent. In 1796 he sold the four houses to the East India Company.

John Bird's three houses

These were clearly once part of the Pembridge's Inn property, but the deed by which William Morton sold them does not survive. By 1636 they belonged to John Bird, who sold them to John Steward, citizen and Pewterer. Steward left the three houses to his wife Elizabeth, who brought them to Captain John Dalby of Ratcliffe on her marriage to him in 1637, and to Edward Hatch, gentleman, on her marriage to him in 1654. At this date the three houses were occupied by Richard Brigstocke, blacksmith, George Bostock, trussmaker, and Thomas Miles, virginal-maker.

In 1660 Edward Hatch and his son Edward sold the houses to Richard and Thomas Kemble. In 1708 Richard Kemble sold them to Joseph Chamberlin, who already held the house immediately to the north. From this date the four houses are treated together, above.

Henry Clitherow's property in Lime Street

Sir Christopher Clitherow's property fronting Leadenhall Street (see p.61) appears to have had a timber house facing the street, with a yard behind, a brick house, possibly the main residence, behind the yard, and a garden and stable, with a gate into Lime Street. Francis More occupied the brick house in 1673, succeeded by Daniel Mercer, merchant, and by 1695 by Mercer's

TWO HUNDRED AND FORTY POUNDS.

LOT II.

AN eligible FREEHOLD ESTATE, fituate in a preferable Part of Leadenhall Street, No. 9, nearly adjoining the Eaft India Houfe; comprifing a roomy Dwelling Houfe, containing Six Bed-chambers, a commodious Dining Room, Kitchen, Shop, Parlour, Yard, and Cellars; the Whole in good Repair, on Leafe to Mr. Thomas Mead, Cane Dealer, for an unexpired Term of 12 Years and a Half from Lady-day 1787, at a very low Rent of per Annum, nett — — — — — — 38 0 0

LOT III.

AN eligible FREEHOLD ESTATE, adjoining the preceding Lot; comprifing a roomy Dwelling Houfe, No. 10, on Leafe to Mr. Wilt, Perfumer, for an unexpired Term of 12 Years and a Half from Lady-day 1787, at per Annum, nett — — 52 0 0

Sale particulars for nos. 9 and 10, Leadenhall Street, 1787. The East India Company may have considered buying these houses but in fact did not, and they did not become part of the site of the new building.

65

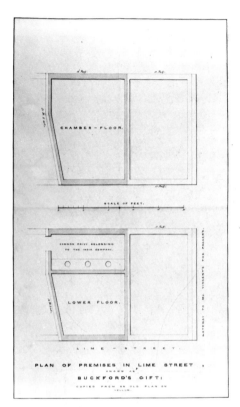

Plan of property in Lime Street belonging to the parish of St. Andrew Undershaft; a nineteenth-century copy of an earlier plan, perhaps of 1722.

widow. In 1695 Henry Clitherow sold all the brick house, yard, and garden to Sir Heneage Fetherston of Hassingbrook. This part now had access only to Lime Street, possibly between some of the houses formerly part of Pembridge's Inn.

The property descended in the Fetherston family. By 1746 it was occupied by Giles Vincent, packer, who was also tenant of Christ's Hospital property nearby. In 1753 Robert Fetherston sold the house to the East India Company. Because of the subsequent redevelopment of the site, before the first detailed plans were drawn, it is difficult to say exactly where this house lay.

Edward Lilley's house

Probably the next house south of the three held in 1636 by John Bird was the one sold by William Morton to Edmund Lilley, citizen and joiner, in 1601. In 1626 Lilley leased the house to John Freebody, gentleman, for 21 years at £6 rent. The house was built over a cellar measuring 20 ft. 4 in. east-west by 14 ft. 8 in. north-south (6.2 m. by 4.47 m.); probably the size of the plot was not more than 26 ft. by 17 ft. (7.92 m. by 5.18 m.). Over the cellar were two rooms on the ground floor, a hall and kitchen above (the latter partly paved, partly tiled), two chambers on the floor above, two more chambers above those, and a garret. The privy was in the cellar.

In 1632 Lilley sold the house to Matthew Billinge, who in 1647 sold it to the leaseholder, Freebody. The freehold descended in the Freebody family, but by 1673 the house was probably occupied by Elizabeth Medlicott. The East India Company were already tenants in 1723, when they bought the freehold from a Mr Freebody. The way in which the Company subsequently developed its Lime Street properties in the eighteenth century is far from clear except for the fact that existing houses were pulled down and unrelated buildings and warehouses erected on the sites.

Elizabeth Turner's three houses

Although it is difficult to determine the relationships of properties on the site developed as warehouses by the East India Company in the eighteenth century, it seems probable that the next houses south of Edward Lilley's, and still part of the same row, were the three held by Elizabeth Turner in the first half of the seventeenth century. They adjoined a tenement held in 1653 by Jane Macroe, sub-tenant of the East India Company, which seems to have been the back part of Lord Craven's property.

Elizabeth Turner left the three houses to her son Edward Burby, D.D., whose son Edward sold them in 1662 to Thomas Buckford. The tenants then were William Dodson, shoemaker, Thomas Roads, clothdrawer, and Jane Walworth, widow; recently they had been Dodson, Godfrey Brimble, musician, and John Walworth, citizen and Merchant Taylor. By his will of 1676 Thomas Buckford left the three properties to his daughter Mary; if she died without heirs, as she had done by 1689, one of the three houses was to go to the parish of St. Andrew Undershaft and the other two to Christ's Hospital.

Christ's Hospital inspected the properties left to it in 1689, and found them to be occupied by John Morris, cobbler, at £8 rent, and Samuel Seamer, barber, at £6, but very much out of repair and requiring considerable expenditure to make them tenantable. A 31-year lease on both houses was granted to Bridget Kent, who was to spend £60 in repairs and to pay £14 rent. In 1720 a new 61-year lease was made to Giles Vincent, packer, at £7 rent; he pulled down the old houses and rebuilt them as one brick house. In 1754, for £1100, he assigned his lease to the East India Company. How long his new brick house stood is not certain; perhaps it was modified rather than demolished to meet the Company's needs. The Hospital sold the freehold to the Company in 1798.

The house left by Buckford to the parish of St. Andrew Undershaft was by 1699 occupied by George Waylett, citizen and Haberdasher. In 1722 a lease

'Colonel' James Turner was a colourful character, and his trial and execution for robbery became something of a cause celebre. Pepys witnessed the execution, which took place near the scene of the crime in Leadenhall Street: '... Kept his countenance to the end ... I believe there was at least twelve or fourteen thousand people in the street'.

Dorothy Greswold   S⟨t⟩ Andrew Undershaft London

NEERE VNTO THIS MONVMENT LYETH BVRYED Y⟨E⟩ BODIE OF DOROTHY GRESWOLD Y⟨E⟩ ONLY DAVGHTER OF ROGER GRESWOLD CITIZEN & MARCHANT TAYLOR OF LONDON W⟨CH⟩ ROGER WAS Y⟨E⟩ 3. SONNE OF RICHARD GRISWOLD OF SOLIHVLL IN Y⟨E⟩ COVNTY OF WARWICK ESQ: SHEE WAS FIRST MARIED TO IOHN WELD CITIZEN & HABERDASHER OF LONDON WHO WAS Y⟨E⟩ 2. SONE OF IOHN WELD OF EATON IN Y⟨E⟩ COVNTY OF CHES= TER GENT: BY WHOME SHEE HAD 4. CHILDREN, VIZ. IOHN ELIZABETH IOAN & DOROTHY: AFTER HIS DECEAS, SHEE MARIED HVGH OFFLEY CITIZEN & ALDER= MAN OF LONDON, & BY HIM HAD ONELY ONE CHILD, VIZ SVZAN AFTER HIS DEATH SHEE LYVED A WIDOW XVI YERES, AND BEING OF Y⟨E⟩ AGE OF LX YERES DYED IN Y⟨E⟩ TRVE FAITH OF CHRIST & HOPE OF E⟨T⟩ERNALL HAPPINES Y⟨E⟩ 29 IVNE 1610

Monument and inscription in the church of St. Andrew Undershaft to Dorothy Greswold (*d.* 1610), widow of Sir Hugh Offley (*d.* 1594).

for 99 years was granted to the East India Company, who subsequently pulled it down and on its site, measuring 13 ft. by 22 ft. (3.96 m by 6.7 m.), built part of its warehouse complex. It was not until later that the Company and the parish realised how unsatisfactory the situation was, with East India House built partly on leasehold land, and the parish owning a freehold which was scarcely identifiable and which it would have great difficulty in reclaiming. In 1832, therefore, some time after the expiry of the lease, and with the approval of the bishop of London, the plot of land was exchanged for a property in Great St. Helen's which the East India Company had bought.

Lord Craven's property in Lime Street

Lord Craven's house (p.58) had its main access from Leadenhall Street, but there was a house at the back opening into Lime Street. In 1653 this back house, consisting of a cellar, five rooms, and two garrets, abutting east on Lime Street and west on the yard of Lord Craven's house occupied by the East India Company, was occupied by Jane Macroe, widow, probably as subtenant of the Company.

The back tenement was included in leases and mortgages of East India House in the later seventeenth century. It was enlarged by the addition of two rooms over the gate in 1670 and let by the Company to Charles Aston, keeper of the Pepper Warehouse. Later it was occupied by the Cashier-General. The freehold was included in the East India Company's purchase from Lord Craven in 1710.

Nicholas Leveson's property in Lime Street

This was the property whose descent in the Middle Ages is traced above, pp.36–7. It was the southernmost of the properties which became part of East India House, later the Lloyd's site, and lay immediately to the north of the alley leading from Leadenhall yard into Lime Street.

Nicholas Leveson held it in 1539. In 1585 William and John Leveson sold the greater part of it to Hugh Offley, citizen and Leatherseller, for £1020. This consisted of a mansion house, already occupied by Offley, five other tenements in Lime Street, and a house of five rooms called the Lodge, formerly part of the mansion house. A small part of the original property remained with the Leveson family; it was acquired by Lord Craven in 1630.

Sir Hugh Offley, alderman, brother of Sir Thomas Offley, lived in the great house until his death in 1594, when he left it to his widow Dorothy, with remainder to his son Thomas. He also left an annuity of £4, charged on all the properties, to the parish of St. Andrew Undershaft, to be spent on bread for the poor and annual sermons. By 1632, if not earlier, the mansion house was no longer occupied by a member of the Offley family. It was leased to Giles Vandeputt, merchant; the other houses were then occupied by two merchants, a cooper, a tailor, a painter, and one of the Town Clerk's clerks. Later in 1632 Christopher Offley, son of Thomas, sold the whole property to Richard Briggenshaw for £1600.

In 1653 and 1661 the great house was occupied by (Sir) Robert Abdy, kt., Bt., but by 1664 was held by John Lawson. Some part of the property seems to have been damaged in the Great Fire, since Richard Briggenshaw paid to have two foundations in Lime Street surveyed by the city surveyor in 1669, the first part of the normal procedure for rebuilding on sites burned in the Fire. By 1667 the great house had been divided into three smaller tenements and sublet. The total rent income from the whole property (nine tenements) was then £179. The freehold descended in the Briggenshaw family. In 1717 Robert Briggenshaw, gentleman, sold the property, described as nine messuages, to the East India Company.

Chapter Four
Lloyd's before Lime Street 1

Detail from Ogilby and Morgan's map of London in 1676, showing Billingsgate Dock, the 'New Quay', and shipping on the Thames.

THAMES STREET

n 35

n 36

n 37

n 38

n 39

n 40

n 41

n 42

n 43

NEW KEY

Chapter Four
Lloyd's
before
Lime Street

In the later seventeenth century London was expanding both as a port for international trade and as a financial centre. The focus for both of these was the eastern half of the city, east of the line of Walbrook. Since the mid sixteenth century overseas trade had been confined to a number of 'legal quays', most of which lay between London Bridge and the Tower, while finance and intelligence centred on Lombard Street and the Royal Exchange. Together they brought captains, merchants, investors, and bankers to this part of the city, and it was inevitable that when a marine insurance market developed it would be located nearby. Even today the precise location of offices in the city is a very significant factor in determining the kind of tenant, and the rent.

The 'legal quays' were already becoming congested by the mid seventeenth century, and one of the few large-scale redevelopments to be successfully undertaken after the Fire was the enforcement of a forty-foot clear quayfront. Nevertheless, the concentration of shipping on this short length of waterfront meant delay, expense, and loss for merchants. It also meant that this area of the city was dominated by services for trade, especially warehouses, and it must also have housed many people with occupations

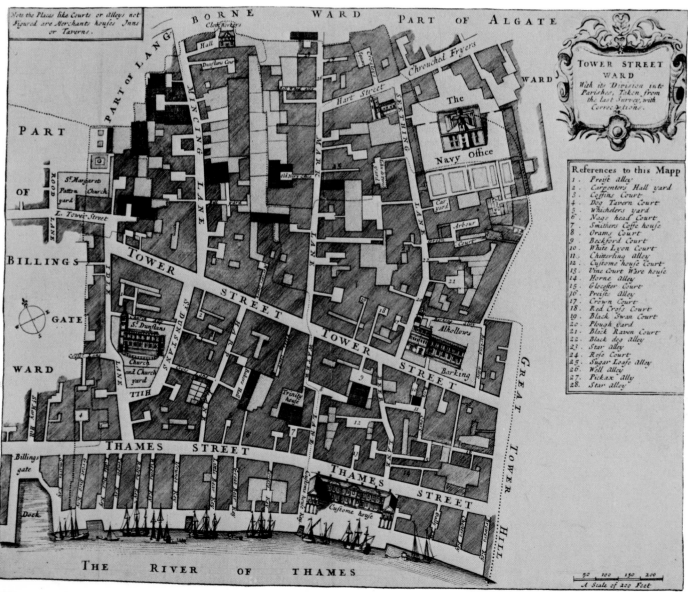

related to trade, shipping, and customs. It was probably this aspect of the area that proved attractive to Edward Lloyd when he opened his first coffee-house in Tower Street, that there would be a large local population, at least some of whom – ship's captains and mariners – would find a coffee-house useful as a centre not only for refreshment, but for news and talk.

Edward Lloyd and his wife Abigail are first known to have lived in London, in the parish of All Hallows Barking near the Tower, in September 1680, when their infant son Edward's burial is recorded. Neither the birth of this child, nor the marriage of Edward and Abigail, is recorded in the parish register, so it may be presumed they had only recently moved there. According to Warren Dawson, an earlier historian of Lloyd's, they lived in Red Cross Alley, near to the church. They remained in that parish until after December 1681, but had moved to the neighbouring parish of St. Dunstan in the East, through which Tower Street runs, by September 1682.

Lloyd's occupation in the early 1680s is not known. He became the proprietor of a coffee-house between March 1685 and March 1687, according to the returns of licence-holders. Unless he had moved meanwhile, this must have been 'Mr Edward Lloyd's Coffee-House in Tower-street' mentioned in a

(Opposite) Tower Street ward *c.* 1754. Lloyd first lived near All Hallows Barking church; the first coffee-house was probably towards the west end of Tower Street near St. Dunstan's church.
(Below) Langbourn and Candlewick wards *c.* 1754. Lloyd's Coffee-house lay on the corner of Lombard Street and Abchurch Lane near to the Post Office.

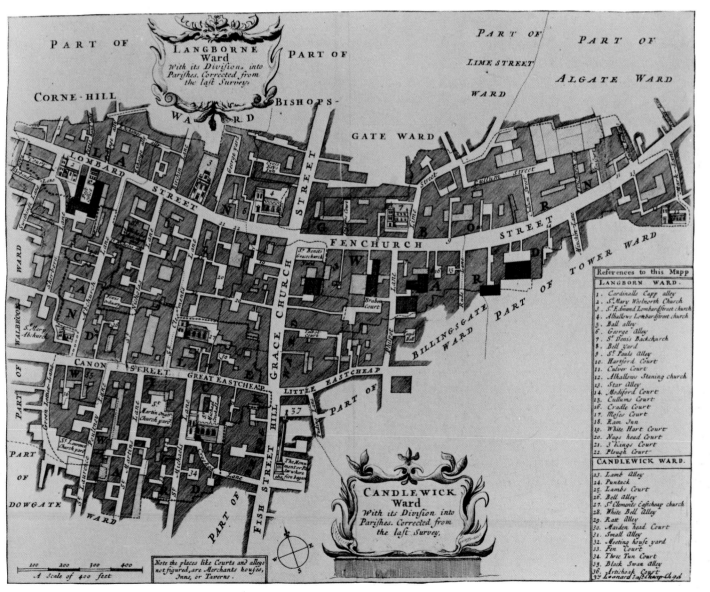

lost-and-found advertisement in the London Gazette of February 1689. The exact location is not certain, but it lay in the Salutation Precinct of Tower ward, probably towards the western end of Tower Street and near to St.

(Above) Part of a list of the inhabitants of Tower ward in 1690, with Edward Lloyd and his household.
(Below) Lloyd's household in Lombard Street in 1695.

Dunstan's church. No details of the building are known; probably it was rented and not freehold, almost certainly it was a new house rebuilt after the Fire, which burned houses all along Tower Street almost to the Tower.

The move from Tower Street to Lombard Street took place in 1691. This was undoubtedly a move into a higher social and business environment, but the maritime connection was not dropped. Although it was some time before the coffee-house became the acknowledged focus of the marine insurance market, recent research has shown that Edward Lloyd was providing shipping information for his customers as early as 1692. This took the form of a weekly newspaper entitled 'Ships Arrived at, and Departed from several Ports in England, as I have Account of them in London. . . (and) An Account of what English Shipping and Foreign Ships for England, I hear of in Foreign Ports'. Publication continued at least to 1704.* Another weekly, called *Lloyd's News*, containing general reports as well as shipping news, was published in 1696 and 1697, ceasing in 1698, but it was the news-sheet 'Ships Arrived. . .' that was the true predecessor of *Lloyd's List*. Proximity to the Post-Office in Lombard Street may have been an important factor in Lloyd's choice of location for his coffee-house.

Lombard Street had, since the time of the medieval Italian merchants from whom it took its name, been a centre for finance, banking, and city business. Before the building of the Royal Exchange, London merchants did business through personal contact and meetings in the street. In the sixteenth and seventeenth centuries goldsmiths, who were also often bankers, congregated in Lombard Street. There were 25 goldsmiths householders in the parish of St. Mary Woolnoth in 1695, though how many of these were bankers is not certain. At the same time the parish held six scriveners, six apothecaries or druggists, and five 'coffeemen', including Lloyd. The rest of the parish, in which there were 85 households, consisted of several victuallers and vintners and numerous small craftsmen.

In 1695 Edward Lloyd's household consisted of himself, his wife Abigail, his two older daughters, three menservants, probably waiters in the coffee-house, one maidservant, and John Finch, probably a lodger but perhaps assisting in the coffee-house. He had two younger daughters, not present in the household at the time of the assessment from which this information comes; perhaps they were out to nurse in a suburban or country village, a not uncommon practice at that time. Edward and Abigail had at least nine children, of whom only four, all girls, survived to adulthood. Elinor, the eldest, later married William Holman, one of the menservants in 1695; Handy, the youngest, married William Newton, then head waiter, in 1713, and they took over the business on Edward Lloyd's death later that year.

There are several accounts and descriptions of the Lombard Street coffee-house. It lay at the west corner of Abchurch Lane, with a frontage both to Lombard Street and the lane; a smaller house occupied the actual corner. The house itself must have been one of the new post-Fire terraced or row-houses, probably of four floors above ground plus cellars and garrets. The coffee-room was probably on the ground or the first floor; an early description refers to wooden tables and chairs and a pulpit from which news and announcements were read. The 'boxes' that formed so characteristic a part of the eighteenth-century coffee-house must have come later.

In the early eighteenth century, after the death of Edward Lloyd, the coffee-house continued to flourish under his name and under the management of his daughter Handy and her first and second husbands, William Newton and Samuel Sheppard. It was still, at least from their point of view, a private enterprise, with no official connection between the management of the coffee-house business and the customers. It was in the early eighteenth century that Lloyd's Coffee-House began to be widely known as a place where marine insurance was available. The Bubble Act of

*I owe this information to Professor John McCusker of the University of Maryland.

Coffee Houses

Coffee-houses appeared in London in the middle of the seventeenth century and continued to be popular places for combining business with refreshment through the eighteenth century and into the nineteenth. 'Boxes' or private booths were not part of the setting at first *(opposite, below)*, but soon became a characteristic feature.

1720, which effectively kept marine insurance in the hands of private individuals, and prohibited the formation of firms and companies to do the same, contributed to the continuance of the coffee-house as the centre of this business; so too did the enterprise of the coffee-house management in providing services for its customers.

From 1734 Thomas Jemson, now master of the coffee-house, began to publish *Lloyd's List*, containing financial news (exchange rates, gold prices, stock values) and news of ships from the ports and abroad. At about this time too the coffee-house gained a great advantage in its intelligence services by compounding with the Post-Office, situated close by, for the free and rapid delivery of reports from its correspondents. This was enormously important to the success of the *List*, and hence to the fame of the coffee-house as a centre for news of marine affairs.

By providing these services the management of the coffee-house ensured its attraction; equally, however, the value of the services to the customers was appreciated by others. If the same services, and possibly better premises, could be provided, then a substantial clientele was certain. This was more or less what happened in 1769, when Thomas Fielding, a waiter from Lloyd's, opened his own coffee-house in Pope's Head Alley, calling it New Lloyd's Coffee-House, and attracted many of the old house's customers. At the same time, though, these customers were able to perceive that it was in their own interests to safeguard the intelligence and other services on which they depended by taking control of the coffee-house business.

In 1771 seventy-nine merchants, brokers, and underwriters, meeting at New Lloyd's, formed the Society of Lloyd's. Almost their first decision was to seek for new premises suitable for their business and their new status. The story of what ensued from that decision is given below.

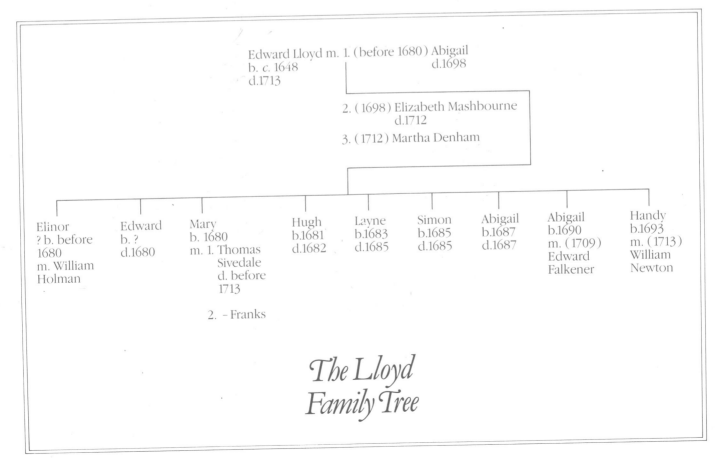

Edward Lloyd m. 1. (before 1680) Abigail
b. *c.* 1648   d.1698
d.1713

2. (1698) Elizabeth Mashbourne
d.1712

3. (1712) Martha Denham

| Elinor ? b. before 1680 m. William Holman | Edward b. ? d.1680 | Mary b. 1680 m. 1. Thomas Sivedale d. before 1713 2. – Franks | Hugh b.1681 d.1682 | Layne b.1683 d.1685 | Simon b.1685 d.1685 | Abigail b.1687 d.1687 | Abigail b.1690 m. (1709) Edward Falkener | Handy b.1693 m. (1713) William Newton |

The Lloyd Family Tree

[Numb. 257.

SHIPS *Arrived at, and Departed from several Ports of England, as I have Account of them in* London; *from* December 15. *to* December 22. 1696.

Falmouth.

Decem. 13. Arriv'd, Spanish Expedition with one Mail, from Corunna.

Plimouth.

15. Sail'd, Daniel of Plimouth, William Athwell, for Cadiz
Mary de Grave of Plimouth, Thomas Harris, for Canary

16. Arriv'd, Van Don & for Flushing. M. Speake, from Guiny
Golden Horse of Dantzick, Jocom Miricom, for St. Ubes

17. John of Plimouth, John Ford, from St. Maloe, with Prisoners

Cowes.

18. Jourfom of & from Rotterdam, P. Andrews, for Plimouth
Peter & Mary, Samuel Osborne | of & for Falmouth,
Alexander, John Simmons——— | from London
With about Ten Sail of Coasters for the Westward

Portsmouth.

15. Arriv'd, the Cornwall, and under her Convoy the Edward
& William, for this Place; and about Ten or Twelve Sail
of Coasters

Fowy.

13. St. Antonia de Padua, John Logotelle, for Amsterdam

Leverpool.

Star, Randal Galloway, from Virginia | last from Ireland
Vine of Belfast, R. Dinwel, from Berbad. |

Harwich.

11. Arriv'd, John & Mary, J. Slinter | from London, for Dantzick
Prince Jacob, John Boy——— |
Sail'd, A Pacquet-Boat | with One Mail | for and from
13. Arriv'd, Bridgman-Sloop ———— | Holland
15. —— | A Pacquet-Boat | ——————— |
17. Sail'd, | ——————— |

At Deal.

14. Sail'd, Upton-Gally, Robert Martell | for Ireland
Edward & Francis ———Jarvey |
Joseph ———Roborham, for Plimouth
John & William ———Harley, for Virginia
St. George Gaity—Bowrey, for Cadiz, & Sail'd the 16th
Sarah ——— Kell, for Ireland
Friend's Adventure ———Piercy | for Canary

21. John & Thomas———Edwards |
William & Thomas———Long |
Friend's Adventure ——— Cumbey |
Colchester-Merchant ——Thompson |
Colchester-Merchant ——Beale— |
Willingmind ———Winicoat— |
Thomas & Francis ——Morley— |

At Deal.

Dec. 16. Castle-Frigate ———Tanner——— | for Canary
Diamond-Gally———Ellis——— |
——————Pennington——— |
Success ———Long——— |
Love ———Well ——— |
Lucy ———Deane——— |
Constant John ——— Dort——— |
Elizabeth & Catherine — Waid |
Resolution ———Gofton |
Sarah & Susan——Harvey——— |
Abigail ———Maynard— |
Anne ———Pine |
Essex ———Wood— |
Providence ———Keeler |
Robert & Nathanael ——— Smith |
Amity ——— Heath, for East-India |

Arriv'd at Gravesend.

15. Friend's Encrease, Roger Golding | from Riga
Providence, William Curling——— |
——————Joseph Jewell | from Narve
Providence, Christopher Western |
Christian Margaret, Henry Griver, from North Bergen
Prophet Daniel, John Muda, from Hambro
Rose-Garland, Aaron Ager, from Stockholm

16. Friend's Adventure, George Philpot | from Riga
Friendship, John Lester——— |
Rose, James Williamson | from Scotland
George, John Hago——— |

20. Lark, Andrew Hawkes, from Lisbon
John & Thomas, Thomas Reynolds, from Narve
Dundee-Frigate, Patrick Fretten, from Scotland
Sea-Aventure, William Godley | from Riga
Paisven, William Paisven— |
Elizabeth, Henry Wisto——— |
Elianor, Michael Harper, from Quenbro
North Star, William Henderson, from Hambro

Sail'd from Gravesend.

17. Herne, Henry Baker, for Legorn
Adventure, Robert Bateman, for Canary

19. St. Michael, Stadefy Govera Coyyo, for St. Sebastian
Boom-Yard, Paul Nelson, for Sound
Post-Horse Christian Priskman | for France
Riga-Merchant, Harman Mowe |

Wind at Three in the Afternoon.

London.		Deal	
December 15. —North-East	December 19. —North-West	December 15. East-North-E	December 19. —— North
16. —North-West	20. —North-East	16. ——West	20. East North-E
17. —North-West	21. —North-East	17. —North-West	21. —
18. —North-West		18. — North-West	

An Account of what English Shipping *and* Foreign Ships *for* England, *I hear of in* Foreign Ports.

Ships in the Bay of Cadiz.

Novem. 12. Thomas & Samuel, Leonard Bowers | for London
Consent, William Clipperton——— |
Elizabeth, Anthony Thorpe——— |
Tree-Hawk, Edward Wills——— |
Elizabeth, Francis Humble——— |
Elizabeth, Thomas Loder——— |
Thomas, Randal Pye——— |
Barnest-Merchant, Richard Wilkey | uncertain whither
Mary-Brigantine, George Cornish——— | bound
Coronation, Henry Roser——— |
Experiment——— | Hacker——— |
Nightingail——— |
Vine, Henry Swinbourne— |
Lamb, Philip Prance——— |
Zant, John Hooper——— |
St. John, John Champion, for Ireland
Lamb-Gally, Matthew Lowth | for Allicant
Provincial, Thomas Burly— |
Rooke-Frigate, Edward Swaine | for Legorn
Tuscany-Gally, George Baily — |
Jesus Maria & Joseph, Tho. de Vardinola | Venicians, for
Jesus Maria & Joseph, Simon de Celrain | London

Arriv'd in the Bay of Cadiz.

14. Macclesfield-Gally ——— Hurle | from Newfoundland
Prince George———Skinner— |
15. Cole & Beane-Gally, J. Hamnell |
18. Richardson-Gally ——— Rider, from St. a Cruise

Sail'd out of the Bay of Cadiz.

Cole & Beane-Gally———Hamnell | for Legorn
Rooke-Frigate, Edward Swaine |
Tuscany-Gally, George Baily— |

Sail'd out of the Bay of Cadiz.

Novem. 18. Macclesfield-Gally———Hurle, for Legorn
Prince George ———Skinner, for Alicant

At Corunna.

Decem. 12. Arriv'd, Spanish Expedition, with a Mail, from Falmouth

Vego.

1. William & John, John Ware | from Newfoundland
Bonadventure, John Corbin |
Isabella, John Jones |
Hare, John Robbins— |
———William Rymer |

Oporto.

Novem. 30. ——— Middleton of Leverpool, from Newfoundland

Lisbon.

William & Daniel, William Bishop | from Newfoundland
Portugal-Merchant, Thomas Sax— |
Gillingham, Colbat Walker——— |
Mary, John Lamprye——— |
Shrewsbury-Gally, John Davison | from Ireland
Frog-Dogger, John Sent——— |

At Mallaga.

13. A Flushinger | for Amsterdam
A Legornese |
City of Mallaga, for Rotterdam
Prince Charles a Suede, for Hambro
Sarah———Suet, for Bristol
Elizabeth & Catherine ———Thorpe | for London
Mallaga-Sloop ———Bearfoot— |
Conception ———Monk |

Arriv'd at Legorn.

Macklesfield-Gally———Hurle; Rooke-Gally ——Swain;
Tuscan-Gally ———Baily
The Ships & Convoys from Smirna, arriv'd at Messina Nov. 15.

The Jeffries, William Cooper Commander, 450 Tons, 30 Guns, bound for *Virginia*, will depart with the *Canary*-Convoy.

LONDON: Printed for *Edward Lloyd* (Coffee-Man) in *Lombard-Street*.

The earliest known copy (15–22 December 1696) of Edward Lloyd's weekly newspaper of shipping information. Publication must have started early in 1692. This discovery was made by Professor John McCusker of the University of Maryland.

Part Two
The Buildings

by
Priscilla Metcalf

Chapter Five
Buildings
Occupied by
Lloyd's
before 1928

Lloyd's rooms overlooking Threadneedle Street
in 1798: the north side of the Royal Exchange,
where Lloyd's gradually took over the upper floor.
In the distance the Bank of England and at right
the tower of St. Bartholomew-by-the-Exchange.
View by Thomas Malton.

Chapter Five
Buildings Occupied by Lloyd's before 1928

About a generation ago, a perceptive underwriter-turned-historian, D.E.W. Gibb, reminded Lloyd's that buildings mould their occupiers. 'The removals from place to place and (between the removals) the perpetual devices to make the same amount of space provide more accommodation ... have influenced ... the character of Lloyd's.' Not only a building, but the institution it houses, he went on, can take new and different shapes on a new site. All down the history of Lloyd's he saw 'environment working on character'. Anyone who wants to understand the modern Lloyd's, he said in the 1950s, must bear that connection in mind. We may think, in the 1980s, that such influences work both ways. An architectural history of The Room tells of environment and character working on each other, partly for continuity, partly for change.

Architecture, Environment and Coffee Houses

The stable element in the story has been made clear by Dr Harding: when port and city were one, the marine insurance market took root near the water. Edward Lloyd's first coffee house in Tower Street can hardly have been more than two hundred yards from the quays 'below bridge', and the Lombard Street house he next moved to was only about four hundred yards from the wharves 'above bridge'. After the docks were built, the captains of ships moored there could proceed under oars to water-stairs within walking distance of Lloyd's Captains' Room at the Royal Exchange. Even during Lloyd's Early Victorian interval at South Sea House, the sounds of London River – and smells too when the wind was right – came from less than half a mile away, blowing along Gracechurch Street towards Bishopsgate. Nowadays the port itself has moved miles away downstream, but communications have changed. Lloyd's shining new crow's-nests above Lime Street can be seen from the ancient river still ebbing and flowing a quarter of a mile away, while electronics bring the oceans nearer – not to mention outer space.

In Lloyd's earliest days described in Part I, the crowded coffee room must have had partly the random air of a public gathering place, partly the inside air of a private club. As time went on in Lombard Street the atmosphere of smoke and stratagems must have reeked more and more of purposeful business. And so, as it began to seem that no ordinary coffee room could contain the insurance market gradually concentrating there, character was restlessly working on environment.

An Unbuilt Design by Robert Adam

Five architects have housed Lloyd's since it emerged from its coffee-house chrysalis in 1773: Edward Jerman posthumously, Sir William Tite, Sir Edwin Cooper, Terence Heysham, and Richard Rogers. The series almost started with Robert Adam.

During 1771–3 there were deliberations, whether to improve the premises in Pope's Head Alley, or whether to build a wholly new and larger Lloyd's Coffee House. Ground was thought to be available at the far end of a cul-de-sac called Freeman's Court, off the north side of Cornhill between Sweetings Alley and Finch Lane. On this plot, owned by Magdalen College, Oxford, stood two ordinary post-Fire houses overlooking on their north side the churchyard of St Benet Fink, Threadneedle Street, a clever little ten-sided church by Wren. The 'Committee for the Building of a New Lloyd's Coffee House' thought the site of these two houses might yield the space required. On 14 April 1772 'Mr Adams produced two plans'. One was for altering the existing coffee house which would cost them £1200 'without any Ornaments at all' and might entail unforeseen 'Expenses and Inconveniences', being 'an

(Opposite) A portrait of Robert Adam (1728–92), attributed to Zoffany. Adam's unused designs for a Lloyd's Coffee House remained among his drawings later acquired by Soane for his museum.

Adam's Designs
for Lloyd's
Coffee House

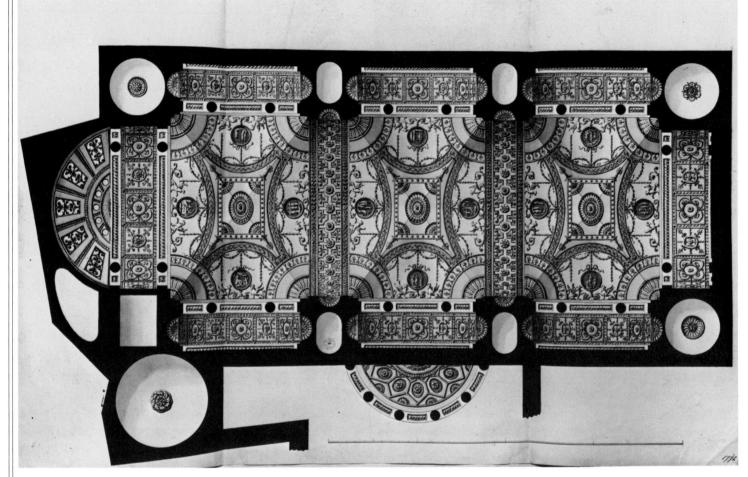

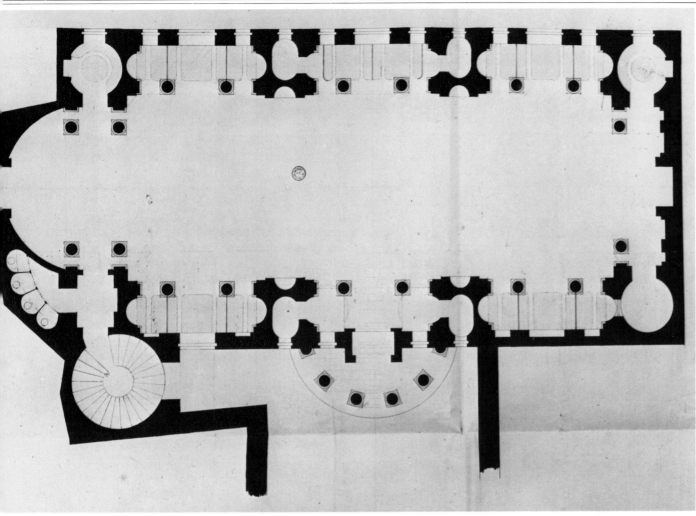

Unexecuted drawings of 1772 for the main coffee room.
(Opposite) The ceiling, and long section looking north. *(Above)* The ground plan (north at the top). *(Right)* End section looking east; the west end is on p. 88. In the alcoves of long section and plan are dimly sketched boxes.

Inside of Lloyds Coffee House

Old Building'.

Their visitor's other plan, 'for the altering and Making the Houses in Freeman's Court into a very Neat and Convenient Coffee House', apparently meant rebuilding entirely within existing outer walls. That would entail buying the sitting tenants' leases of which he gave precise details. 'Mr Adams', so named at the eight committee meetings he attended between April 1772 and June 1773, acted as the committee's agent treating with tenants and the steward of Magdalen College. Architects then were not above this, although Robert Adam, presumably the one involved, already had aristocratic clients and himself sat as M.P. for Kinross. We take it that he was the brother chiefly concerned because the surviving drawings are clearly his, but it is possible that James Adam was the member of the firm who came to committee meetings and did the dog's-body work.

In the Soane Museum are five handsome drawings for what would have been Lloyd's first custom-built premises, long before they finally built for themselves in the 1920s. Of external design little could be made of a façade among close-set houses, save for a semicircular entrance porch at the head of Freeman's Court. The interior was the thing. The entire ground floor was to consist of one big room, about 75 feet long including an apse at the west end intended to take advantage of a jutting-out of the site. The half-dome over the apse was to be partly studded with little skylights – very hard to clean outside they would have been. Three great triple Venetian windows were to overlook the churchyard, each triple opening wholly – not just centrally – surmounted by a fully glazed lunette, a trick Adam could have adapted from Robert Taylor's new Bank of England court room, an equally deep space needing all the light it could get. For Adam's windows were to be set off from the room by little alcoves – unusual in his other work – for semi-private business talk. In these alcoves dimly indicated coffee-room boxes can be made out on both plan and section. Little circular corner rooms, two of them with fireplace and seat, could be even more private. Walls and the vaulted ceiling were to be elaborately decorated in Adam's best 'embroidered' manner (ready no doubt to develop marine motifs in two dimensions, as his Admiralty screen on Whitehall does more sculpturally). In short, he brilliantly metamorphosed common coffee-house decor into his latest West

Adam designed the west end of the room with a half-domed screened apse.

(Above) A later riverside view of the Adam brothers' Adelphi development off the Strand. *(Below)* The courtyard of the Royal Exchange in the middle of the 18th century.

End style, which he was then applying to Derby House in Grosvenor Square.

The irregular end bit of ground allowed not only for a set of water-closets but for a separate entrance and staircase to regions above and below. Kitchen and servants' quarters will have been intended for the basement, and committee rooms upstairs, with upper floors tentatively also for housing a displaced tenant – fertile source for trouble. Nevertheless, the great coffee room would have fortified the prestige of this loosely organized group of men.

But 'Mr Adams' negotiated in vain, new-building may have seemed too bold then, the committee wavered. And in 1773 more suitable premises were available, as we shall see. Eventually Freeman's Court was to disappear in the clearance of 1842–4 for enlarging the environs of the new Royal Exchange. The spot once occupied by those two houses lies beside the pedestrian way east of the present Royal Exchange, mostly under the north end of Royal Exchange Buildings near the site of St. Benet's where the Peabody statue is. If Lloyd's had built here, they could have stayed at most seventy years, doubtless overflowing periodically into neighbouring houses – the insurance market's needs for space tending ever to inflation.

This was not the first coffee house Robert Adam designed: his British Coffee House in Cockspur Street near Charing Cross, a gathering place for his fellow Scotsmen, dated from 1770. But his Lloyd's Coffee House would have been one of very few works by him east of Temple Bar. The most fashionable British architect of his day was seldom a City of London architect. So far as we know, none of Lloyd's committee had been his client before. (But one of them, John Whitmore, was soon to engage him to design a house in Old Jewry, adjoining a housing development by the Adam brothers in Frederick's Place.) To the Adam brothers as architects on the make, impelled by the demands of maintaining a large office, especially just then – for their Adelphi scheme failed in 1772 – the Lloyd's job though comparatively small would have been the right advertisement at the right time to the right people, men of affairs likely to want larger houses or to vote money for new building works. Even hidden from the world at the end of a cul-de-sac, the splendid room as centre of business intelligence and investment would have fortified the architect's prestige as well as theirs.

But some Lloyd's men saw that a cul-de-sac was not the place for an enlarging body on its way to becoming an institution. Premises were available in the Royal Exchange, that conspicuous address near the Bank of England and the Mansion House, antedating them both. So Lloyd's men postponed architectural patronage for later generations. And in August 1774 'Messrs Adams' were paid £150 'for Surveying & Drafts'. So much for architectural prestige. Quite by coincidence Lloyd's today possesses an Adam room, not at all *in situ*, as we shall see.

Lloyd's First Term at the Royal Exchange, 1774–1838

In November 1773 a lease was signed between Lloyd's committee and the Gresham Committee (of the City and the Mercers' Company as joint landlords) for rooms previously occupied by the British Herring Fishery Society 'over the Royal Exchange', and the move was made early in 1774. Incidentally, the chief instigator of the move, John Julius Angerstein – one of Lloyd's truly great men – was then himself employing an architect George Gibson Jr for his own villa at Greenwich, now a library on Mycenae Road. From 1787 Angerstein's town house was in the West End at 100 Pall Mall, until his death in 1823 housing the art collection that was to be the nucleus of a National Gallery. City men no longer felt the need to live over the shop. London was expanding, spiritually and physically.

The Royal Exchange Lloyd's moved to was the second on the site, the building of 1667–71, its famous original having been destroyed in the Great Fire of 1666. The original Royal Exchange had been founded a century before the Great Fire by that energetic Londoner Sir Thomas Gresham, modelling it on the exchange at Antwerp as a place for merchants to meet in, and bringing workmen and some materials for it, marble and glass and panelling, over in his own ships. Until then London merchants met to do business out in the open in Lombard Street. Gresham's Exchange, as centre of mercantile intelligence, came to be called 'The Eye of London', perhaps also partly because it was built round a courtyard open to the sky in the middle. The 'wooden O' of the Globe theatre across the river might be called

This caricature of Lloyd's coffee room at the end of the 18th century conveys a sense of the humming business there.

Elizabethan London's other eye.

The Elizabethan Exchange set the basic quadrangular shape for its successor on the site: two main storeys around a courtyard, the ground floor with shops entered from the street and the upper storey, also with shops at first, reached by stairs to long internal galleries. Under these galleries loggias surrounded the courtyard, like the covered arcaded walks around an Italian square, and so these English walks came to be called piazzas, although the Italianism came via Flanders. In 1666 'the fire ran around the galleries' upstairs, creating a horrid precedent that ought to have been a warning to their rebuilders. Even in the third Royal Exchange built after the fire of 1838, the central courtyard, with covered walks around, itself remained uncovered and open to the sky until the 1880s, despite forty years of petitions from the less robust citizens complaining of draughts. The primitive spontaneous street-market idea of business in the open air was thus perpetuated for a surprisingly long time at the Royal Exchange, although the brokers of the Stock Exchange were meeting indoors in the eighteenth century and the insurance market, as we have seen, began to come indoors for its shipping news in the seventeenth.

Each rebuilding of the Exchange enlarged its site. Gresham's building faced Cornhill, while an uneven row of houses lay between its north side and Threadneedle Street. The second building had its towered main front on Cornhill and a porticoed north front partly protruding into Threadneedle Street, which is not parallel to Cornhill. The designer in this case was Edward Jerman the City Surveyor, of a dynasty of master carpenters experienced in the City, and surveyor also to the Fishmongers' and Goldsmiths' Companies. In two crowded years after the Fire before he died of overwork in 1668, he supervised and apparently designed the rebuilding of several livery company halls as well as the Royal Exchange, and directed the felling of timber in Berkshire for barging down the Thames to a city hungry for building materials. The Exchange was completed by the mason Thomas Cartwright with a monumental entrance tower in the spirit of the new City gates such as Moorgate which he was rebuilding at the time. Merchants were allowed to return to the courtyard in 1669 while hammering still went on around them

Pugin and Rowlandson's view of Lloyd's rooms around 1800 shows clock and wind-dial, skylights and notice boards, enquiry desk and barrier, and the coffee-room boxes in action.

(though shopkeepers could enter their shops only in 1671), and the City was once again 'on Change'.

When Lloyd's moved in in 1774, it had two large rooms, plus kitchen and committee room, on the upper level, at the west end of the north or Threadneedle Street side. The rest of the upper floor was then occupied mainly by Royal Exchange Assurance Company offices and East India Company warehouses. Sanitary arrangements consisted of a request to the East India Company to share the pipe to their cesspool – none of the elegant soap-dishes and ivory-tipped taps for hot and cold of the 1840s. But there was some embellishment of the two coffee rooms with 'new lustres' to improve the lighting and new copper ventilators in the windows and new lamps on the staircase to the street: light, air, and the 'way in' – the perennial problems. And there was construction of boxes. The historic box seating of successive Lloyd's rooms perpetuates the table-flanked-by-high-backed-benches formation in public eating and drinking rooms, first remarked in print of coffee houses in 1712, though the old word 'box' had been used for a small separate room in a tavern on City craftsmen's plans of the 1680s.

The two coffee rooms, one for subscribers and one for the public, seemed less large almost immediately. Expansion began along the north side in 1786. In 1791 former premises of the governors of the merchant seamen's hospital were converted into another subscribers' room. In 1802 still another subscription room, formerly occupied by the commissioners of stamps, was added, so that three communicating rooms were strung out along the whole north side of the Exchange, while the original subscription room became an additional coffee room for non-subscribers having business with subscribers. The original public coffee room of 1774 or Blue Room was used chiefly for ship sales and known by 1803 as the Sale Room and before long (at any rate by 1812) as the Captains' Room. The bar or panelled-and-balustraded barrier, between subscription rooms and a lobby where enquiries could be made, is shown in the Pugin Sr/Rowlandson view, as well as the coffee-house boxes already lengthened to take six men instead of four each as stipulated in 1774. The coffee room with skylights Pugin showed will have been an inner room, for there were apparently no windows on the courtyard side; and the skylight was a fact of life for Lloyd's in the next Exchange too. The presence already of clock and wind dial, so important to estimates of arrival under sail in London River, must be noted. A sparse but elegant decor is faintly suggested by Pugin as background to Rowlandson's busy lively figures, assured in every sense, Lloyd's men going about their business. In November 1800 when Nelson 'was upon the Royal Exchange some time', there apparently took place Lloyd's presentation to him of silver to honour his latest glorious victories, silver services of which certain pieces have since found their way back to Lloyd's.

As Lloyd's expanded along the upper floor of the Royal Exchange, the fitting up and altering of the rooms was in the hands of successive surveyors to their landlords the Gresham Committee: in 1774 Emanuel Crouch of whom nothing else is known save his years as the Mercers' surveyor, succeeded by a John Baker, and he in 1787 by Richard Jupp, surveyor also to Guy's Hospital and to the East India Company as we shall see later, and the renovations of 1802 were under 'Mr Lewis', probably James Lewis, surveyor also to Christ's Hospital and to Bridewell and Bethlehem Hospitals. The network of such surveyorships was always thick in the City. But Jerman's Royal Exchange was not built for the ages. Its outer walls of stone and its presumably brick-vaulted cellars enclosed a completely timber-framed and wainscotted structure, all resting on shallow foundations. In 1767, a century after it was begun, Parliament voted money for heavy repairs, the west side having to be almost completely rebuilt. By 1812 Lloyd's premises were riddled with dry-rot requiring more repairs. In 1820 the Gresham

Committee's surveyor George Smith had to rebuild the Cornhill gate-tower and the main staircases. As other nineteenth-century occupiers discovered of large City buildings reared in a hurry after 1666, seventeenth-century foundations were not damp-proof. Nor was the Exchange any more fireproof than its predecessor had been.

The nature of its construction was cruelly exposed one windy freezing night in January 1838 when the entire building except for the new tower and old outer walls burned to the ground. Unpublished minutes of the enquiry set up by the Gresham Committee recorded the testimony of Bank of England night staff and late passers-by who rushed to the rescue shortly before eleven o'clock. The alarm was raised when the Bank's watchmen on duty opposite the northwest corner of the Exchange saw firelight in its first-floor windows, then smoke and sparks pouring from the roof, and the Cashier ordered out the Bank's engine. All fire cocks were found to be frozen until doused with warm water, doubtless from the watchmen's tea-kettle. Next the parish engine dashed up and attended to its parishioners' shops, though they were not burning yet. Meanwhile the Exchange's iron gates were broken open and the Fire Brigade arrived (already directed by James Braidwood, who was to die in the Tooley Street fire of '61). Witnesses described the race of flames through the wind-tunnels of the first floor galleries and roof spaces all undivided by party walls, and then below the galleries the lath-and-plaster vaults of the piazzas burning round the courtyard to either side of the stone tower which stood while its bells crashed from their wooden beams.

View from Cornhill of the fire that destroyed the Royal Exchange on the night of 10–11 January 1838.

Those first into Lloyd's secretary's office found only the cornice on fire, and were able to save most of the minute books, after a little misunderstanding with the firemen about looting, before flames took over. Similarly in the Subscribers' Room at first the fire was only playing along the ceiling, so that some drawers of papers could be saved. But those first on the scene found the Captains' Room and its kitchen burning too fiercely to be entered, so it was there that the fire must have started. The kitchen had had an ordinary fireplace, with range, boiler and hot plate adapted to the uses of a coffee room (not yet a restaurant kitchen) and the chimney had been recently swept: the Gresham Committee interviewed the surveyor-in-charge and the chimney-sweep, as well as those responsible for the nightly closing of the rooms. It was concluded that the building was 'badly constructed' and that no individual was to blame. Except for the fires that destroyed the Houses of Parliament in 1834 and the Albion Mills at Southwark Bridge in 1791 (covered by Lloyd's, which handled fire risks by then), this was London's worst blaze since 1666. An entirely new Royal Exchange was required, and almost seven years were to roll by before Lloyd's could move into it.

Interval at South Sea House

By 1838 Lloyd's business was so central to the City's business that interruption was not to be thought of. Proprietors of near-by premises were

South Sea House as rebuilt 1723–7 at the east end of Threadneedle Street, north side facing Bishopsgate Street. Lloyd's lodged here during 1838–44 while the Royal Exchange was being rebuilt.

quick to offer temporary space. The fire occurred in the night of 10–11 January. On the morning of the eleventh the underwriters squeezed into a room at the Jerusalem Coffee House, favourite haunt of East India merchants, in Cowper's Court off the south side of Cornhill just west of Birchin Lane while, in the London Assurance boardroom in Birchin Lane, Lloyd's committee pondered what to do next. For a week from 12 January Lloyd's business was transacted in several rooms at the London Tavern on the west side of Bishopsgate near Cornhill where the Royal Bank of Scotland later stood. This hostelry, since rebuilding in the 1760s, was so grand, visitors mistook it for the Bank of England, and lavish within though of dignified simplicity outside. Just then, early in 1838, the shareholders' meeting held there in chapter two of *Nicholas Nickleby* was occupying Dickens's mind.

Arrangements more lasting were made for the underwriters' use of rooms at South Sea House, a large courtyard building at the east end of Threadneedle Street, north side just off Bishopsgate Street, later occupied by the Baltic Exchange, rebuilt 1902 as British Linen Bank, later Bank of Scotland. Apparently the sleepy atmosphere of South Sea House, before Lloyd's woke it up for a while, was much the same as when Charles Lamb wrote of it (in 1820 looking back on his short time there around 1790, before his long stint in East India House): in this 'melancholy-looking, handsome, brick and stone edifice ... some forms of business are still kept up, though the soul be long since fled', in offices like 'state apartments in palaces', with long worm-eaten tables, that have been mahogany, with tarnished gilt-leather coverings, supporting massy silver ink stands long since dry ... [and] vast ranges of cellarage under all, where dollars and pieces of eight once lay ... long since dissipated' by the 'breaking of that famous Bubble'. In fact, the speculative South Sea mania had burst in 1720 upon this building's predecessor, and South Sea House was entirely rebuilt during 1723–7 to the plain Palladian design Lamb and later the men of Lloyd's knew. The architect had been the South Sea Company's surveyor James Gould with masonry work by his son-in-law George Dance Sr, later the architect of the Mansion House. The great hall at South Sea House, for which Lloyd's hired tables and benches (their boxes having been entirely consumed in the fire), could seat only 232 underwriters to the 320 previously seated at the Royal Exchange, and Lloyd's secretary with his clerks had to occupy a South Sea Company official's house in South Sea Passage next door.

The Captains' Room had to be accommodated separately, not so much because the South Sea Company disapproved of its coffee-house ways, but for lack of suitable space – yet perhaps between the lines we may sense some faint horror of its kitchen as the Gresham Committee enquiry into the late fire proceeded. So for the first year and a half of exile the Captains' Room was accommodated by the City of London (sometimes called New London) Tavern, another spacious hostelry grandly rebuilt, with giant pilasters dignifying its long front at the bend of Bishopsgate Street, east side, opposite the end of Threadneedle Street and so just over the road from South Sea House. Then in June 1839 other licensed premises had to be found for the Captains' Room, farther along Bishopsgate Street on the west side, opposite St. Ethelburga's church, and there it stayed, still only a few minutes walk away yet inconveniently not under Lloyd's roof, until all could re-enter the Royal Exchange together.

So Lloyd's spent the first years of the new reign in exile from the site where it had been putting down roots as an institution, though this was a vigorous exile during which considerable reshaping of its working arrangements went on. Considerable reshaping of London itself had been going on during the earlier years of the century and especially during the reigns of George IV and William IV, with the making of new roads and new bridges, new squares and new buildings. A spirit of renewal was in the air.

And then in Victoria's Coronation year the City's financial heart held an empty blackened site crying out for renewal and for widened approaches – no new challenge to a generation that had seen the making of the docks, the shaping of Trafalgar Square and Regent's Street, and the approaches to a new London Bridge.

The Rebuilding of the Royal Exchange 1840–4

After an architectural competition that was ill-managed and controversial (like many another Victorian architectural competition, and some modern ones), William Arthur Tite was appointed the architect for a new Royal Exchange. The powerful design of his main rival in the affair, Charles Robert Cockerell, architect to the Bank of England and Professor of Architecture at the Royal Academy, would have provided a much nobler building, but Tite won. He was a man of the City, having grown up in Fenchurch Street (at no. 80 east of Northumberland Alley, south side, where his father was a Russia merchant), started school in Tower Street and later was articled to the architect David Laing near by, helping him in his rebuilding of the church of St. Dunstan-in-the-East (once Edward Lloyd's parish church). Tite's own first office was around the corner in Jewry Street, Aldgate; subsequently he established himself in St Helen's Place, Bishopsgate, where he produced his drawings for the Royal Exchange. And so, for any little conferences with the secretary of Lloyd's on the plans for their new rooms, South Sea House lay on his way to the site.

Tite's work by then included Mill Hill School (Greek Revival), the Scotch Church, later Irvingite, Regent Square (Gothic Revival), the Golden Cross

The Victorian City and its approaches.
(Below) London Bridge looking north *c.* 1900 (before the pavements were widened and parapets balustraded), when the traffic was thick but the skyline was low.
(Opposite above) The river with barges and warehouses, looking upstream to London Bridge in the 1870s.
(Opposite below) The Bank intersection at the heart of the City *c.* 1897, with the Royal Exchange, home of Lloyd's, surrounded by horses.

LONDON BRIDGE. B-1064.

Tite's Plan

(Above) Arcade designed by Tite in 1842 for the public lobby or vestibule of Lloyd's rooms at the Royal Exchange.

(Below) His plan for Lloyd's rooms (north at right). 'Private rooms' for the north end of the Underwriters' Room were apparently not built, and the doorway there was replaced in the 1850s by a second arcade (on plan opposite and on p. 100), removed in 1883 to add the vestibule to the Room. The Captains' Room during 1844–54 occupied the corner rooms at lower right. The Commercial or Merchants' Room west of the lobby was later the Reading Room, later still the Brokers' Room. The 'Merchants' Area' was the open courtyard below.

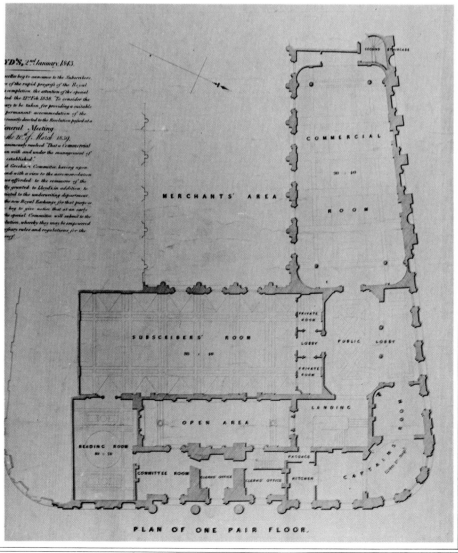

Hotel at Charing Cross, replacing the one known to Mr. Pickwick, and sundry terminals such as railway stations and cemetery chapels – nothing on Cockerell's noble plane, but in tune with their time. Tite also had something to do with the London & Westminster Bank in Lothbury, in junior partnership with Cockerell in 1837–8: while it is often said of that building (since rebuilt) that Cockerell designed only the outside and Tite did the inside, it is clear from the contract drawings that Tite had very little to do with it. Cockerell's skill in using classical elements to unite disparate interior spaces was the civilizing language Sir Edwin Cooper was to deploy for Lloyd's in the 1920s. Tite's talent was a scenic skill in mixing styles – a quality some historians have unkindly called 'plastic bombast' – but he mixed them with great dignity and practicality. His Royal Exchange has the last big classical portico in central London (that is, apart from the one on Spurgeon's Tabernacle at Elephant and Castle), its back-and-sides and court façades are neo-baroque, the bell-tower (on the east this time, crowning Lloyd's entrance) is neo-Wren, and Lloyd's rooms were 'in the Venetian style enriched after the best Roman models'.

Yet Tite's builder, Thomas Jackson, had the latest in high technology, such as travelling cranes moving on elevated rails to lift heavy blocks of stone (one of which in a strong gust of wind was 'precipitated into the street'). Such

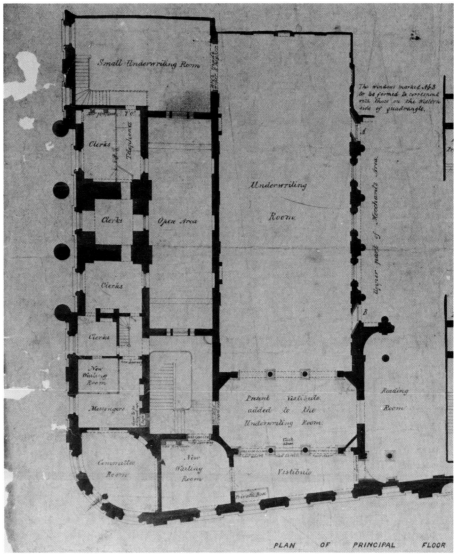

Plan of Lloyd's rooms as they were in 1882 (north at bottom), before alterations in 1883. The Reading Room at lower right, replacing the Merchants' Room in 1855, housed rows of giant ledgers. The Captains' Room, moved in 1854 to rooms west of that (off right), had been succeeded at the lower left corner by the Committee Room and a new waiting room.

machines were being used on other prominent buildings, such as the Houses of Parliament, and earlier on the Reform Club. Now the Royal Exchange has come to be a symbolic part of the scenery here at the central junction of streets with Dance's Mansion House portico and the rebuilt remains of Soane's Bank of England. Tite's portico provides a Roman backdrop for the Duke of Wellington's equestrian statue installed at the intersection then recently cleared of buildings. Street-widening north and south, and clearances on the east regularized the Exchange site into a trapezoidal shape which Tite adapted for the ground plan of his building, widening it eastward so that Lloyd's premises at the east end were, as required, larger than the Royal Exchange Assurance premises at the west end. He retained the mainly two-storey elevation and enclosed courtyard of Gresham's and Jerman's buildings.

From the pedestrian walk east of the Royal Exchange one approached Lloyd's first-floor rooms through the gateway under the clock-tower, where a big lamp on graceful iron supports and iron tracery saying 'Entrance to Lloyd's' filled the head of the arch. One then turned right in the (then) open light-well behind the tower, to Lloyd's own doorway and stone staircase. Lloyd's two main rooms lay L-wise on two sides of the central courtyard, and between them lay a big vestibule divided by an arcaded screen into a side space used at first as a cloakroom and later as a lobby, and a main circulating space. The secretary's and clerks' rooms were in the range under the bell-tower, animated by vibrations from above.

A picturesque feature of Tite's interior design and typical of him was an architectural flourish that appeared in many a view of the Room (as the underwriters' room came to be known): the tall triple arcade forming the north side of the main vestibule space, and also for a while its mirror image, a second triple aracade forming the south side of the vestibule at the head of the Room (the latter arcade inserted after Lloyd's moved in, probably in the mid-1850s, and abolished in 1883 when the vestibule space became part of the Room). Such triple-arched screens were a favourite neoclassical motif, often on porches or staircases, framing entrances. The first one here may also have been meant to recall the arcades of Gresham's and Jerman's courtyards.

View of the Room, probably in the 1870s, looking south from the vestibule through the second arcade, inserted in the 1850s to echo the original one on the north side of the vestibule and removed in 1883.

THE LATE SIR W. TITE, C.B.

Here each of the free-standing supports was a single Doric column on a high base, each column carrying its own fragment of full entablature. Such singling-out of the elements of a classical order like an exemplar in a builder's pattern book – that is, with the entablature not continued from one column to another – characterized various eighteenth-century London works Tite would have known first-hand or in reproduction. He was perhaps drawing on and recombining the varied handling of such features by Sir Robert Taylor at the Bank of England (Transfer Offices, demolished by Soane, and the Court Room where the columns are paired), and also by Sir William Chambers for the staircase of Carrington House (originally Gower House in Whitehall Place, demolished 1886). Tite would have absorbed the former from Malton's views of the 1790s, the latter from Soane's Royal Academy lectures (illustrated by drawings, long before lantern-slides) in Tite's pupil days. Stored as new in a young architect's sketchbook, to be brought out of stock as needed.

Tite's main assistant on the Royal Exchange was an architect named Charles Ferdinand Porden, who had supervised the building of St Pancras church for the Inwoods and had himself designed St Matthew's Brixton before spending ten years in Tite's busy office, where there is no reason to suppose he initiated any part of the Exchange design, so important was it to Tite as head of the office.

The Royal Exchange of 1840–4 was indeed his chief claim to fame. Never a top-flight architect, Tite was a person of importance in his day: Liberal M.P. for Bath 1855–73, President of the R.I.B.A. 1861–3, 1867–70, knighted 1869, C.B. 1870, magistrate, bank-director, hospital-governor, committee-sitter. He appears briefly again in our story financing a transaction in Leadenhall Street. He had antiquarian interests, was a Fellow of the Society of Antiquaries, and was said to have a large library of English literature. He was in some respects not unlike Lloyd's future architect Cooper, who designed big offices for City grandees and collected English watercolours on the side. Tite in his later days lived well in Lowndes Square and was heard telling the Prince of Wales that he had inherited a fortune, married a fortune, and made a fortune. How different from the seventeenth-century craftsmen-designers of the previous

(Above) William Arthur Tite (1798–1873).
(Below) Sketch of Lloyd's lobby or vestibule in the *Illustrated London News* (probably by John Gilbert) during Queen Victoria's visit to open the Royal Exchange in October 1844. Looking east to the stair landing, the then doorway to the Room is at the right and the original arcade at the left.

Royal Exchange.

Sovereigns came whenever the Exchange rose or fell: Elizabeth I in 1571 to see Gresham's completed building and declare it Royal; Charles II in 1667 to lay the first stone for a new one among its blackened ruins, as Prince Albert was to do in 1842: and finally Queen Victoria in 1844 to open the third Royal Exchange. That was the occasion for a tremendous banquet, it being ever a City custom when celebrating a new building to invite celebrities to dine in it. Before anyone moved in, the banquet was held in Lloyd's own rooms as the largest rooms there. All too few members of Lloyds, it was irritably felt at the other end of Threadneedle Street, were invited, the demand being so great. But the day after Christmas 1844 Lloyd's left the increasingly cramped hall of South Sea House and moved into what seemed to be splendidly large quarters at the Royal Exchange where they were to remain, increasingly cramped, until 1928.

The Character of the Room, 1844–1928

Here in these Early Victorian premises more fully evolved the idiosyncratic nature of 'The Room' – Olympian title – where the accolade was to be called 'a great man of the Room' or, even better, 'born in the purple of the Room'. The insurance market known by then all over the shipping world as Lloyd's consisted essentially of underwriters seated in their boxes, or market stalls, and brokers circulating among them to place their risks, like customers shopping for a best buy. Or, the place was a cross between an exchange or trading floor, with dealers on their feet, and an open-plan office with experts sitting down. The atmosphere had the spontaneity of the marketplace. Underwriters were not employed by Lloyd's, which was a society of individuals. The society employed staff – descendants of the coffee-house

The royal banquet in Lloyd's Underwriting Room to celebrate the opening of the Royal Exchange in October 1844, before Lloyd's boxes and their occupiers moved in in December. As in the view on p. 100, the actual space was much inflated by the artist.

waiters – to make the market and its marketplace work. Architecturally the marketplace was of mixed parentage too. The Royal Exchange had late-medieval merchants' exchange/town hall/cloth hall origins, but we are concerned with the rooms occupied by Lloyd's in the third Exchange, moulded by other models too.

A pattern adopted for some of the grander trading floors in early nineteenth-century Europe, instead of the market hall or exchange, was the Roman basilica with internal colonnades and top-lighting so that outer walls could be clothed in columns too or, on crowded sites, in other buildings. Such models were variously adapted for stock exchanges during 1800–10 in St Petersburg, Paris and London. But the open-plan office must have appeared first in the banking halls set up in the tall-windowed rooms of Italian palaces. London's eighteenth-century versions at the Bank of England designed successively by Sampson, Taylor and Soane increasingly partook of basilican patterns too. The basilican model and the palace model for public rooms gradually merged.

Meanwhile another office type developed as a series of small rooms: the kind of office originally set up in private houses, when City men still lived over the shop, or in former private houses let off as offices with resident housekeepers. The purpose-built 'stack of offices' for letting to more than one tenant at a time occurred sooner in the City than one might think, an early example going up in Clement Lane about 1823, presumably in ceiling-height and window-size scaled to the neighbouring houses. (When warehouses multiplied vertically they too were known as 'stacks of warehouses'.) So, as building-type, the small Victorian office or counting-house was descended from the private house, in origin quite separate from the large-halled Victorian office modelled on the public building of basilican or palatial pattern.

The Late Victorian Room and its prevalence of top hats. The brass basket at the end of each box was for delivery of policies for signing, before a Signing Bureau was invented to deal with them.

Lloyd's Boxes and Ledgers

(Above) The Late Victorian Reading Room.
(Below) The vestibule looking west, after widening of the doorway in 1906 and adding of brokers' boxes in 1912. Loss Book at left, rostrum and Lutine Bell at right.

(Above) The Captains' Room as spaciously depicted in 1844. The reality, both here and as housed during 1854–1928, was more crowded. *(Below)* The Room after expansion at its south-east end in 1906, looking north.

Lloyd's early operations went on for almost a century in domestic-size rooms built at a time when coffee-house keepers plied their trade at home. Only when Lloyd's operations became more complicated and organized, attracting many more people, did it need to move to rooms built on a public scale. And large-scale the Room has been ever since – except for its determinedly small-scale boxes, which no other office, large or small, ever had. (Even in palatial Late Victorian restaurants, successors to the old coffee houses, women's evening dress needed individual seats.) The feature that distinguishes the Room from other open-plan offices is that the gangways tend to be as crowded as the boxes, because this is a trading floor too. Mixed parentage can produce unique offspring.

All these people in the Room at the Royal Exchange – underwriters and their staff, brokers and their staff – were Londoners, many in the Early Victorian years still living in the City, as time went on more and more of them coming from farther and farther out but considering themselves men of the City, and so their memories of life at the Exchange tell too of the Victorian, Edwardian and neo-Georgian City outside. John Bennett the first Secretary of Lloyd's (d. 1834), living at Tooting Common, rode to and from Lloyd's on horseback. Still in the 1860s a few still rode into the City, others drove and put up at the livery stables then standing at all approaches to 'the stones'. One reminiscer aged 80 in 1925, who had started in his father's brokerage office in 1864, recalled how his father used to ride in on horseback from Leyton, sending on his groom by bus. An underwriter, whose father had been elected to Lloyd's in 1825, remembered in 1922 his own sixty years there, when he came in from the suburbs by bus, too crowded for reading a newspaper, but one could obtain it from a waiter perambulating the aisles of Lloyd's with an armful of newspapers – dispensing the news as in the eighteenth century a waiter would read it from the coffee-house pulpit. This same underwriter in his last years in the 1920s arrived daily at Lloyd's in a horse-drawn brougham (Lloyd's had then been insuring motor cars for ten years). Still in 1938, Lloyd's oldest subscriber attended a City church twice on

Travelling to Lloyd's

London transport during Lloyd's days at the Royal Exchange.
(Opposite) A growler, the public cab version of the private four-wheeled brougham. On this page, buses, trams and hansom cab.

Sundays although he lived in northwest London.

Their business being worldwide, these men's horizons went far beyond the City. As a journalist said of the Room in 1859, 'not a breeze can blow in any latitude, not a storm can burst, not a fog can rise, in any part of the world, without recording its history here'. This chamber, that has been called 'a whispering gallery of the world's accidents', was no mean place, although its actual adequacy to the business varied. Its predecessor, called in 1791 'the most perfect suite of any in Europe appropriated to commercial purposes', was remembered after its destruction in 1838 as dark, dingy and proud of its discomforts. Tite's new rooms were praised in 1844 for their fitness to the 'exact wants of a great trading community', but inconveniences arose within the first ten years.

There had been two miscalculations in planning, not by the Gresham Committee or its architect, for Lloyd's as principal tenant had been carefully consulted. These concerned the presence of the Merchants' Room, or Commercial Room, in the second of Lloyd's two large rooms, and the placing of the Captains' Room. The former grew from an idea that would have been less powerful if the traditional courtyard of the Royal Exchange had not been temporarily wiped out and then left unroofed thereafter. The idea also gave rise to a private speculation that flourished briefly near by: Moxhay's Hall of Commerce (1842–9) in Threadneedle Street on the sixteenth-century site of St Anthony's Hospital, present site of the National Westminster Bank. It was really the old mercantile-exchange idea that had impelled Gresham. The Merchants' Room was meant to be a meeting place for bankers, ship-owners and other businessmen paying an annual subscription of two guineas each, a sort of commercial club-room. It was, at first, thought advantageous to Lloyd's to have them around, and possibly disadvantageous to have them somewhere else. It was not a coffee room, but the Captains' Room was open to them. The Merchants' Room formed the main part of the north range of the Royal Exchange, with its south windows overlooking the courtyard. In each corner a decorative column pretending to support the vaulting conferred dignity and minimum interference with business. But the very presence of so much space unavailable to the all-too-soon overcrowded underwriters became an interference, and the Merchants' Room was abolished in 1854. It then became the Reading Room, so that some underwriters could move into a projecting bay off the far end of their Room that had served originally as a reading room, with an upper gallery for Admiralty charts. This small Underwriting Room came to be known, for its distance from the head of the Room, as Botany Bay. The new Reading Room with its banks of ledgers and files of newspapers later provided seats for brokers and, later still, telephones.

In the mid-1850s too, the meeting place and refreshment room for ships' captains was moved. At first in 1844, received back into the centre of things after separate exile in Bishopsgate Street, the Captains' Room occupied three connecting rooms at the curved northeast corner of the first floor, with a nice view of the passing scene on pavements below and a small kitchen with serving-hatch tucked in alongside. Entry was by Lloyd's front stairs and main vestibule. Stairs, vestibule and cloakrooms thronged with habitués of the Merchants' and Captains' Rooms cannot always have assisted the underwriting business. In 1855 when another tenant's premises beyond the west end of the new Reading Room fell vacant, the refreshment room was transferred there, where an existing staircase from Threadneedle Street, and from 1883 an hydraulic lift, gave separate entry. Entry of another sort to the Captains' Room was stopped by wire traps outside windows to the courtyard: against rats climbing up in search of food – like the rat guards on mooring ropes of the captains' ships. And so the Captains' Room kitchen was once more a bit of a hazard.

Entrance from Threadneedle Street to the Captains' Room lift. At left inside was the Enquiry Office (plan on p. 111).

Just inside the Threadneedle Street entrance there was arranged in 1883, beside the lift, a sliver of ground-floor space with a narrow counter for an Enquiry Office, sometimes jokingly called Lloyd's Missing Persons Bureau. Here relatives of ships' officers and seamen could come for news. When ships were long absent Lloyd's with its intelligence network would know first where and how they were. A new boy in 1885 later remembered being initiated into posting with quill pens in different-coloured inks, in massive ledgers on long lectern-like stands in the Reading Room, 'the arrivals, sailings, speakings' of ships reported by telegraph from Lloyd's signal stations and agents then increasingly stationed about the world. When in 1928 these ship-movement ledgers, going back to 1828, were replaced by card-index cabinets, the *Daily Mail* called them 'giants of the City', or dinosaurs. One end of each of the two main rooms had a wind-dial controlled by a gauge on the roof, still then used for estimating arrivals under sail in the river, and a clock synchronized by private wire from Greenwich Observatory. Clock and wind-dial had been features of Lloyd's earlier premises, but by 1925 only six sailing ships were registered at Lloyd's, and a few (modestly) taller buildings in the City were beginning to make their own local winds.

Linked though the Room was with exotic distant places, it had its own local problems of light and air and temperature and noise. At first the only windows to the Room itself were three opening on to the still unroofed

(Above) A ship-sinking is entered in the Loss Book.
(Below) Reading Room ledgers as pushed back against the wall in 1912 to make room for brokers' boxes.

(Opposite) Charles Barry Jr's glass roof for the Royal Exchange courtyard, installed in 1884 (*Builder,* 13 Oct. 1883). It limited light and air to Lloyd's first-floor windows (upper right and behind us).

(Below) The Threadneedle Street entrance lobby as altered 1883. At left, Lloyd's Enquiry Office, where seamen's families could ask for news of ships. At right of the lift, a bench for telegraph boys.

courtyard, and a set of clerestory windows in the raised central part of the ceiling. Subsequently windows were made in the east wall into the area or light-well between the Room and the tower, and when the courtyard's new glass roof in 1884 further dulled the light, more skylights and windows had to be made. For artificial light by the 1880s there were gas 'sun-burners', making new heat-and-air problems, and in 1885 electricity was introduced in the main rooms. But the clerical offices still used oil-lamps then, and kept a precautionary supply of brass candlesticks, each with 'Lloyd's' stamped on a corner of its square base. As for the twin problem of ventilation, around one o'clock all windows were opened for half an hour, though by three or four when crowding was greatest there was a most memorable stuffiness. Big detached marble-topped fireplaces stood one at the far end of the Room, others in the Reading Room, and in the 1880s–90s a stove with a clock on it stood in the vestibule at the head of the Room. On hot summer days pans with great blocks of ice were placed in the gangways between the boxes.

All day long in the Room there was the background hum of voices and the sound of 'incessant tramping … the traffic being very great', 'a continuous shuffling and scraping of feet' remembered as 'very disturbing'. Dickens's brother-in-law Henry Austin said he paved Lloyd's floor there in 1844, probably with some stonelike composition. Pitch-pine floors were later tried, and in 1913 a rubber floor-covering was laid (with canvas put down where the index clerks worked to protect it from ink spots). But there were far more insistent noises. The bells in the clock-tower immediately overhead played (and still play) well-known tunes, different for each day of the week, at nine, noon, three and six o'clock. The bells were remembered with nostalgia by many. Others remembered trying to catch a telephone message

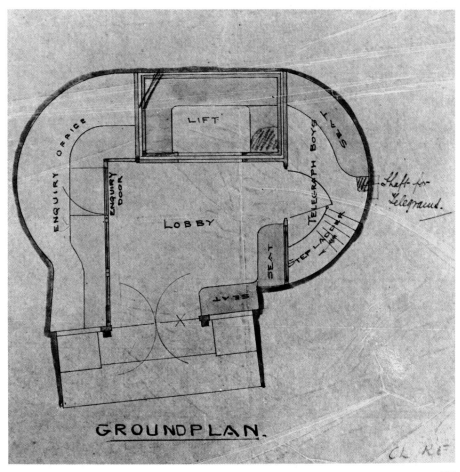

GROUNDPLAN.

'amid the din created by thirteen monsters overhead' and 'sultry afternoons when ... one solitary blong-g-g would crash forth from the belfry at seven minutes to three, this being the final note ... omitted from the preceding Sunday's hymn tune'. There were legends that in 1838 the old bells had pealed out 'There's Nae Luck aboot the Hoose' until they crashed down, and that the bells in 1915 greeted the first Zeppelin raid with 'Oh Dear! What Can the Matter Be?'. Be that as it may.

The Room's most characteristic sound came to be the voice of the caller, or crier, at the head of the Room calling out the names of brokers wanted by visitors at the barrier. Men whose memories went back to the 1860s–70s, when entrance directly into the vestibule was a left turn from the stair-landing, recalled that one man was both doorkeeper and caller, and there was no rostrum. Lloyd's greatest caller, Walter Farrant, who dominated the Room with his magnificent voice and patriarchal beard from 1879 until 1913, received his pulpit in, it would seem, 1883 when the geography of entry to the Room was altered during heavy renovation work by the firm of William Cubitt. The new way-in went straight ahead off the landing through a lobby (former cloak room) and then through an arch of Tite's triple-arched screen into the vestibule that now formed the head of the Room. According to the committee minutes of 1883 'the position of the Crier' was about to be 'experimentally established' in January and in March was fixed 'between the door in the Screen ... and the stove'. When the doorway to the Reading Room was widened in 1906, the rostrum was moved nearer to that. The mahogany rostrum now in the Museum of London incorporated a seat like a throne with a high back pragmatically (and uniquely?) curving over as a sounding-board. It was probably made in 1883 in the Cubitt workshops in Grays Inn Road, though no exact record remains. While not dating back to the new building of 1844, it carried on the tradition of the eighteenth-century coffee-house pulpit from which ships were sold and waiters read out the news, as described by Addison and Steele. Still in the Victorian Captains' Room a special 'high desk' was brought out for ship sales, until 1895 when the sales were moved to the Baltic Exchange. The underwriters' rostrum at the Royal Exchange was retired in 1928, after an active life of less than fifty years, to be superseded at Lime Street by one of greater size and an elegance of quite different origins.

The famous Lutine Bell has been closely associated with successive rostrums, yet when Farrant first had to silence the Room for special announcements he used a hand-bell. At that time a ship's bell, kept as a trophy at Lloyd's after its retrieval from the sea in 1857, rested under a table in the waiting room outside the Secretary's room. It may have been the Secretary, Colonel Hozier, keen on perfecting communications in general, who thought of mounting this bell in a decorative framework beside 'the Crier' in 1897, when the committee minutes record an order for making the frame. The bell, inscribed 'St. Jean', perhaps its patron saint, and '1779', is thought to be from the French frigate *Lutine* built at Toulon dockyard in that year, captured by the British and in 1799 sunk off the coast of Holland while taking money from London to Hamburg, insured by Lloyd's (the broker being Angerstein). Since 1897 its deep clear note has been sounded for important news relating to ships overdue and for other momentous news, for the visits or deaths of sovereigns and great men, and on Lloyd's own special occasions. As a 'trophy of triumph over the ocean' the Lutine Bell has become a symbol of Lloyd's. How appropriate that Billiter Street next door traces its name to bell-founders once settled there.

More mechanical communication arrived. Hozier, who was responsible for first extending the network of Lloyd's signal stations and cared much about improving efficiency at home, is said to have carried out his office duties 'with the aid of speaking tubes'. Memories of Lloyd's first telephone

(Opposite) Walter Farrant, the Room's patriarchal caller 1879–1913. He received his pulpit in 1883 (now, Museum of London) and the historic Lutine Bell for special announcements in 1897. Photographed after his rostrum was moved nearer to the Brokers' Room doorway in 1906.
(Below) The bell as installed 1958–86.

The Lutine Bell

(Right) As installed (with a length of anchor chain) at the Royal Exchange in 1897.
(Lower right) As installed in the rostrum at Lime Street (west) in 1928. (*Lower left*) as installed on the rostrum at Lime Street (east) in 1958.

box as a place of torment in the 1890s were recalled fifty years later by a one-time broker's boy – the waiting in line and then turning the handle, the conversation fading just as one was connected while the other boys tapped on the glass. By the end of 1914 there were twenty-six telephone boxes in the Brokers' Room (as the Reading Room was by then more often called), with switchboard – the operator shouting to the rostrum when someone in the Room had a call. And there were shouts from the barrier to the rostrum when someone in the Room had visitors. The din was reduced in 1925 by installing a telewriter system from the barrier and the switchboard to the rostrum, by then fitted with microphone and loudspeakers. But still in 1927 the *Daily News* spoke of pandemonium at Lloyd's that no ordinary businessman would tolerate. Yet all this masking noise could ensure the privacy of a conversation.

In the mid-1920s London's telephone exchanges were 'going automatic', one could no longer pick up the phone and say 'Lloyd's', one had to ask for Avenue 7100. During the first World War the General Post Office would telephone to Lloyd's if an air-raid was expected and everyone on the premises would proceed sedately to the basement (where the printing machines for *Lloyd's List* had been set up in 1914), and if the all-clear call seemed unduly delayed the Secretary, Admiral Inglefield, would walk over to the G.P.O. to see what was up. All very inconsequential compared to 1940.

Various statues and monuments were part of the scenery at the Royal Exchange, the most arresting that of William Huskisson M.P., who died in 1830 as the world's first victim of a railway train: symbol of a new risk but dressed in a Roman toga, eleven feet tall with pedestal and all in white marble, by the sculptor John Gibson. It was given to Lloyd's in 1847 by Huskisson's widow, whose drawing room was not high enough to take it without a hole in the ceiling (so that, it was said, the presence of the marble head under her bed became unbearable to her). By 1915 Lloyd's, being too pressed for space to keep it, gave it to the London County Council to be set up in Pimlico Gardens at the river end of St. George's Square. And there was

Looking east in the vestibule in 1897. At left the newly installed bell, the clock on the stove, and the rostrum. At centre, statue of Huskisson, *d.* 1830 as the railways' first victim, apotheosis of a new risk.

the memorial to Lloyd's war dead, designed by Sir Edwin Lutyens and unveiled in 1922 by Field Marshal Earl Haig. It framed the entrance to Lloyd's room on the main staircase landing, lighted by the glass dome over the stairwell, the whole of the wall flanking the door recess being faced with marbles in greens, greys and white, with pilasters bearing the names flanked by marble flags, and a tablet and cartouche with Lloyd's crest above. The memorial was moved to Lime Street in 1928 to a somewhat crowded position

Memorial to Lloyd's war dead 1914–18, designed by Lutyens, carved by Derwent Wood, unveiled 1922 by Field-Marshal Earl Haig. This main first-floor entrance to Lloyd's rooms from the stair landing had been remodelled since the plan on p. 99.

outside the Room, and is being set up again in the new building.

Soon after that war a Lloyd's chairman presented a flagpole which was installed on the roof over the Committee Room at the north-east corner of the Royal Exchange, and Lloyd's ensign was flown from it in business hours. That Committee Room with its odd quarter-circle plan (reflected in the table made for it) had been briefly the heart of the Captains' Room of 1844–54 along with the rooms either side of it, until removal to new quarters west of

(Above) Lord Haig at the rostrum on a visit to Lloyd's in 1920.
(Below) A view of the Room showing skylights over the first-floor rooms at the Royal Exchange as in the 18th century on p. 91.

the Reading Room. The Captains' Room after 1855, with its skylighted bar and its chop-house boxes on a smaller scale than those of the Room, and its nautical memorabilia on the walls became, more and more, simply a restaurant for Lloyd's – especially after ship-sales ended in 1895, its salty flavour more and more of a memory. It could only serve about two hundred lunches a day, but its habitués loved it, for it filled a need which connoisseurs of the geography of offices will understand: it was a meeting place, part of the intelligence network. Or so its supporters insisted in 1920 when expansion in the numbers of staff threatened its existence, for Lloyd's premises had now become desperately inadequate. This was no longer only a marine insurance market but accepted fire, burglary, employers' liability, motor and now even aviation risks. The Intelligence Department, for one, was working under shocking conditions, the Committee thought. The great Captains' Room issue was really the first airing of problems that were to lead to Lloyd's removal from the Royal Exchange altogether. The manoeuvres that accomplished this belong in the next chapter. It should be mentioned – as even architectural historians are sometimes confused – that Lloyd's Registry of Shipping, housed since 1900 in a handsome building by T.H. Collcutt in Fenchurch Street, is an entirely separate institution.

From the giant ledgers of the Royal Exchange, *below,* to the card-indexes of Lime Street, *above.*

Lloyd's announced in December 1923 that they were to build on the major part of the old East India House site at Leadenhall and Lime Streets. Purchase was completed in June 1924 and the site was cleared of the Victorian 'congeries of offices' known as East India Avenue. The new foundation stone was laid by George V in May 1925, and in March 1928 the King came back to open the new building. Lloyd's moved in at Easter time. The last day at the Exchange on Maundy Thursday, 5 April 1928, was celebrated by 'hilarious scenes' and the chairman's speech from the rostrum heralded by the Lutine Bell.

The mahogany boxes of the Room at the Royal Exchange, their backs raised by glass partitions against draughts and noise, with brass-wire cages fixed at each end for policies delivered by a rugby-scrum of brokers' clerks, were to be replaced by new teak boxes still on the old lines. The archaic and the new were to proceed together. The old Room was mourned by many as 'like a club'. The influence of geography, of whose box was next to whose, was thought to have been more felt there. But character and environment would undoubtedly continue to work upon each other in the new building some three hundred yards up the road. A few prophets already said Lloyd's would outgrow that one too.

From the toppers of the Royal Exchange (as on p. 103) to the bowlers of Lime Street, *below*.

Chapter Six
Architecture in the Lime Street Area before 1978

St. Hellen:

St. An

THE BRIDGE

To return to forerunners in Lime Street: London's skyline *c.* 1600 as glorified by Visscher in 1616. He may never have seen London but infused other men's panoramas with legendary grandeur out of English seamen's tales. St Andrew's tower marks the neighbourhood where an East India Company was then germinating and about to take root on Lloyd's future Lime Street site.

St. Dunston in the east

Lion Key   Billings gate

Chapter Six
Architecture
in the
Lime Street Area
before 1978

Lloyd's new site was rich in marine associations. For more than two centuries the core of it was the seat of the Honourable East India Company, also known as the United Company of Merchants Trading to the East Indies, whose councils directed the chain of trading posts from which grew Great Britain's Indian empire, and whose fleets of fast-sailing East Indiamen brought cargoes of tea, indigo and pepper, silks and cottons to the company's warehouses in London. Here to 'the India House' came great soldiers who served the company, Lord Clive, the Duke of Wellington, Lord Cornwallis and Earl Canning. And the company employed, either in India or in Leadenhall Street, men like James Mill and John Stuart Mill, Macaulay, members of the Strachey family, Thomas Love Peacock, and best known of all, Charles Lamb.

The East India House

Despite the picturesque overtones of the place and increasing collections of Oriental art within, the architectural aura of this site for 250 years was to be mainly classical. That is, if we date the use of the classical tradition here from the East India Company's Palladian rebuilding of the 1720s, followed by a century of additions in the same taste, next by the grimly basic classicism of Victorian offices that replaced it, and finally by the huge classicism of two interlocking buildings that stood here for fifty years in the twentieth century. The ovals and circles of Richard Jupp's ground-plan of 1796–9 for East India House and Sir Edwin Cooper's ovals and circles of 1924–8 for Lloyd's and the Royal Mail Steam Packet Company came out of the same tradition.

As for earlier buildings on the site described by Dr Harding, wherever renovation occurred in the seventeenth century there appeared the style called artisan-classicism – exuberant, incorrect, playing with classical elements – common on City façades such as those surviving until 1800 next to the west end of East India House. But the late seventeenth-century gatehouse-front of East India House itself was another matter, its upper part painted like a billboard with a great view of ships to honour the Coronation of 1661, a special-occasion piece, despite its date completely medieval in spirit. If it lasted into the 1720s, the change of façade style there then will have been as sudden as that of the 1870s farther east when Norman Shaw introduced his Queen Anne Revival for a Victorian shipping company at 34–5 Leadenhall Street.

The East India merchants chose as architect in 1726 a comfortable merchant closely related to another trading community, a young man who took an informed amateur interest in what was then modern architecture. (This was one of those moments when men of the City employing architects for business or for country houses expected the latest modern style – revival though it might be.) Theodore Jacobsen, born probably at Hamburg, came of a family of German and doubtless also Danish origin, that had been for several generations masters of the Steelyard in London, representing the traders of the Hanseatic League here; he succeeded his brother as 'house-master' in 1735. Their uncle Theodore gave to All Hallows the Great (the Steelyard's parish church) the carved screen now in St. Margaret's Lothbury. The East India Company had warehouses at the Steelyard, a compound of buildings near Dowgate by the river (later supplanted by Cannon Street Railway Station).

It is clear from surviving evidences of the design approved by the company in March 1726 that its designer was familiar with avant-garde books such as Colen Campbell's *Vitruvius Britannicus* of which the third volume came out in 1725. (Theodore Jacobsen should not be confused with Sir Theodore Janssen of the South Sea Company, a subscriber to *Vitruvius Britannicus* and an amateur of the Anglo-Palladian style.) Jacobsen was later

(Opposite) East Indiaman at sea.

123

to design the Foundling Hospital, Captain Coram's foundation that was to be endowed by the works of Hogarth and Handel. Jacobsen's portrait was painted for the hospital by Hudson; he was also painted by Hogarth (a portrait now at Oberlin, Ohio); and he became a Fellow both of the Royal Society and the Society of Antiquaries. He died 'at a great age' in 1772, and may have been in his mid-thirties in 1726. As he was not an experienced architect, the East India House building works were directed by John James, a seasoned architect who practised also as a surveyor.

The surviving evidences of Jacobsen's design include views of the Leadenhall Street front in c. 1760 and 1795, and interior views published after 1800 of rooms not affected by building works in 1796–9, as well as a plan drawn before those works began. The front of the new building was flush with the pavement, unlike Craven House behind its gatehouse, and the new frontage more than twice that of the old ship-painted front. It was five bays wide and three main storeys high with a fourth concealed at the top, and the ground floor was treated as a rusticated and arcaded basement for a Doric order of very flat pilasters embracing the first and second storeys, its entablature crowned by a balustrade. Into the arches of the ground floor were set straight-headed door and window openings with heraldic carving over the windows – this last as on the garden front of Marshal Wade's house built in (Old) Burlington Street in 1724 to an influential design by Lord Burlington (based on a Palladio drawing he had recently acquired in Italy) published in the 1725 volume of *Vitruvius Britannicus*. Compared to

Leadenhall Street looking east *c.* 1795. At right, East India House as designed by Theodore Jacobsen in 1726, shown just before rebuilding began in 1796.

Burlington's highly modelled elevation, Jacobsen's was low-key and even a bit lifeless, yet in the City it was certainly an early exercise in the new Anglo-Palladian series, about six years before George Sampson's richer front for the Bank of England. The South Sea Company were also rebuilding at the time but externally very simply without an order. The giant-order-on-a-basement formation had of course been introduced to London a century earlier by Inigo Jones, and then exploited by artisans (Lindsay House, Thanet House), revived by Wren and loosely applied by men like Robert Hooke, for example on the Merchant-Taylors' School in Suffolk Lane near the Steelyard. Jacobsen could have been updating something he was used to.

His most interesting room inside was apparently unusual in its day. The Sale Room, also known as the amphitheatre, was called the Old Sale Room after 1799 and clearly pre-dates the rebuilding completed then, a plan of it having been made before that work started and, indeed, its early eighteenth-century ironwork leaps off the page of Pugin's drawing published in 1808. Pugin the French refugee, father of the Gothic architect, arrived in London via Wales and Nash's office in 1796, and may have made his original drawing as background for Rowlandson's figures then. On plan the room was slightly trumpet-shaped, narrowing towards the railed dais, with rows of seats rising away from it either side of a central entry, and the room was two storeys high.

For precedents outside the City adapting Roman amphitheatres to indoor use, one thinks of Palladio's theatre at Vicenza and Wren's Sheldonian at Oxford. In the City there was the much more centralized anatomical theatre

Leadenhall Street at the corner of Lime Street looking west in 1802, with East India House as rebuilt and extended eastward by Richard Jupp in 1796–9. In the distance at right the Green Gate houses, demolished before 1806, and the churches of Cornhill beyond.

London. Printed for Bowles & Carver, No. 69 St Paul's Church Yard.

A View of the EAST-INDIA HOUSE, Leadenhall Street, London.

Richard Jupp Esq. Architect.   Published 26 Feb 1802.

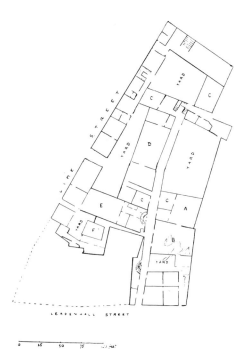

by Inigo Jones for the Barber-Surgeons' Company, a room much venerated by Lord Burlington, and there was Hooke's domed octagon for the Royal College of Physicians: these demonstration theatres had to be centralized. One suspects a commercial source for our sale-room amphitheatre, rather than some lecture-theatre (although Adam's lecture hall for the Royal Society of Arts in the 1770s may imply a precedent of that nature), for we are not talking of the semicircular pile of boxes of contemporary entertainment theatres or the more modest stepped forms of contemporary schoolrooms. Plans of the Steelyard before and after the Great Fire include no such room. What did the Dutch East and West India Companies provide in Holland then in this line, likely to excite emulation? Or the Hanseatic League in Hamburg?

Notice too, this Sale Room's Anglo-Palladian statuary niches and garlanded clock, and the great skylight over the dais. Skylights as a contribution to London living – over staircases in Savile Row in the 1730s for instance, and upper rooms in the eighteenth-century Royal Exchange – were a feature of contemporary architectural design. Nineteenth-century views of the Sale Room, when it was dignified by meetings of the company's court of proprietors, show more niches added probably by Cockerell or Wilkins. But the sales held there were far from dignified. The tea sales, according to Knight's *London* in 1843, 'are yet remembered with a sort of dread ... the uproar became quite frightful' and could be heard even over the market noises in Leadenhall Market. Survivals from Jacobsen's building later removed to Whitehall by the India Office included fittings of the Directors' Court Room, paintings by George Lambert and Samuel Scott of Calcutta, Madras and other ports, and a marble chimney-piece by Rysbrack showing Britannia receiving the offerings of India. Jacobsen's rooms were demolished in 1861.

In 1754, when East India House expanded to the south, additional offices were designed by the company's surveyor William Jones. Jones's chief distinction was that he had been architect at Ranelagh, the pleasure gardens on the Chelsea side of the river, rival to Vauxhall on the south side. His Rotunda of 1742 was an original building (long before Wyatt's Pantheon in Oxford Street; indeed the Albert Hall has been compared to it). Canaletto's

(Above) Ground plan of East India House drawn just before rebuilding began in 1796, showing Jacobsen's building at lower right. Room A was his Directors' Court Room (shown below). Room B was his Sale Room (shown opposite).
(Below) The Court Room in the 19th century, looking south, with Rysbrack's chimneypiece of 1730 at left.

East India House

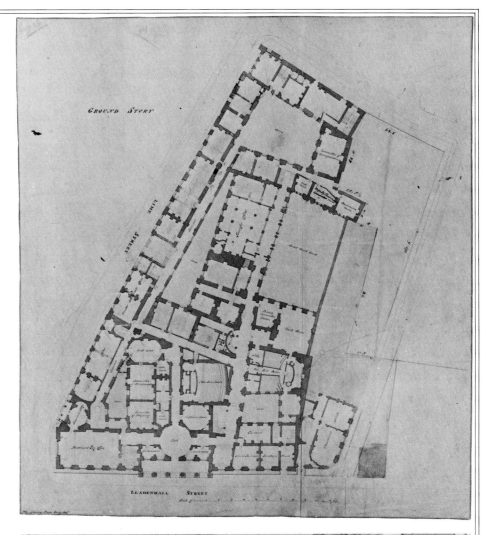

(Above) Ground plan of East India House drawn in Holland's office in 1806, showing Jupp's rebuilding of 1796–9 and Holland's addition at the west end after removal of the Green Gate houses. The Old Sale Room (room B on plan opposite, and below) is shown with its banks of seats and dais.
(Below) The Old Sale Room, built to Jacobsen's Palladian design in 1726–9, as drawn by Pugin and Rowlandson for publication in 1808.

view of its interior hangs in the National Gallery. Jones himself was painted by Hogarth. Early in this architect's career he published *The Gentleman's or Builder's Companion*, a book of rococo designs for gates, pavilions, chimneypieces, etc. The unrecorded character of his East India offices may have been less rococo than those.

After Jones came Jupp as surveyor to the company 1768–99. Richard Jupp and a brother were the first generation of architects in a family of master craftsmen and pillars of the Carpenters' Company. He was one of the original members of the Architects' Club, founded in 1791 as a first step towards the organization of the profession, a membership requiring travel in Italy and France. His was the design for the famous porticoed long front on Leadenhall Street of the East India Company's last sixty years. It was to offices in this

Jupp's New Sale Room of 1796–9 (to the left of the old one on plan, p. 127) in use as part of the Company's museum, before and after redecoration in the 1850s by M. D. Wyatt.

building that the elder Mill and Peacock were appointed in 1819, and from here Lamb retired in 1825, having started work in the older building in 1792, and from here Macaulay departed for India in 1833.

Jupp's design of 1796, mainly executed 1797–9, was partly a refronting of Jacobsen's rooms as a west wing, partly a rebuilding around those rooms, and partly new building on newly acquired ground embracing the Lime Street corner. The ground-plan of the place thereafter shows the, by then, deep site riddled with light wells and courtyards, though Lamb wrote of 'light-excluding, pent-up offices, where candles for one-half the year supplied the place of the sun's light'. This was already the London of coal-smoked fogs, especially so near the river. But Jupp's planning was far more elegant than Jacobsen's. Behind the portico he placed a big circular lobby, from Lime Street a smaller circular lobby gave entry to the Seamen's Pay Office in the east wing, and there were various ingeniously curved rooms as well as a top-lit, galleried New Sale Room, later part of the company's museum.

Jupp's new front, on such a narrow way as Leadenhall Street, was usually seen sidelong in its new length, yet the six giant Ionic columns of the portico flanked by generously spaced wings, even though the whole was only two storeys high, had something of the grandeur of a seat of empire – which it was. That idea was celebrated by the sculpture of the great pediment, executed by John Bacon: Commerce introducing Asia to Britannia at whose feet Asia pours out her treasures, defended by George III with the City barge, for some reason, in the background, and the pediment surmounted by Britannia seated on a lion, Europe on a horse, and Asia on a camel – allegories well on their way towards the Albert Memorial.

Another deep site near by was under reconstruction at the time: the Bank of England, by the brilliant young architect John Soane, Jupp's fellow-member of the Architects' Club. In 1796, before the East India Company had decided on an architect, it seemed Soane might have that commission too, until Jupp reminded the directors of his long service and implored them to commission him, which they did. There was more room for the play of Soane's brilliance on the Bank site: if he had arrived at India House, Jacobsen's rooms might not have survived as long as they did. When Jupp died in 1799 most of the work was finished, except for interiors completed by Henry Holland and subsequent additions on west and south. Working drawings for the building now in the Victoria and Albert Museum had been kept, naturally enough, in Holland's office as he had to settle the accounts, but they clearly relate to Jupp's time. An album of interior details by Holland is in the R.I.B.A. Drawings Collection.

After 1800 there was further building at the west end by Henry Holland, to make living quarters for company officials, as a semi-attached house (later part of the ever-growing museum) elegantly curved back to keep East India House clear of lesser buildings beyond it. (Long delay in clearing title to a small patch of ground at the northwest corner of the site may account for Holland's backswept design here.) By the time Holland succeeded Jupp as surveyor to the company, he was one of London's most fashionable architects. (Such surveyorships as these kept an architect in touch with potential clients.) His work included Brooks's Club in his early thirties, the remodelling of Carlton House for the Prince of Wales, Drury Lane Theatre for Sheridan, and sundry country houses including Claremont for Lord Clive in collaboration with Holland's father-in-law 'Capability' Brown.

Next on the scene after Holland died in 1806 came Samuel Pepys Cockerell, sometime surveyor also to the Foundling and Pulteney estates, the Victualling Office, the sees of Canterbury and London, and St. Paul's Cathedral, and highly original architect of St. Martin Outwich church which used to stand opposite South Sea House, also of the surviving tower of St.

A seat of empire reduced to an auctioneer's handbill.

Anne's Soho, and country houses including Daylesford for Warren Hastings and Sezincote in Anglo-Indian style for his own brother (who had made a fortune in the East Indies, and their sister married Hastings' secretary, so the Cockerells were well placed). S.P. Cockerell at this time was assisted by his son, later the greater architect, C. R. Cockerell. At East India House the work the Cockerells were in charge of in 1822–3, on the west side of the site south of Holland's addition, had unhappy consequences: subsidence, possibly caused by inexperienced use of the newest high technology of the day, cast-iron beams. So S.P. Cockerell despite his connections had to resign in 1824, to be replaced by William Wilkins, who some years before had designed the East India Company's college at Haileybury.

By 1824 Wilkins had already done a number of notable buildings such as Downing College, Cambridge. In London within the next ten years he was to undertake University College, St. George's Hospital, and the National Gallery in his cool Greek style. For East India House, besides rebuilding Cockerell's work he designed more offices in 1828 on newly acquired ground at the southwest of the site. East India House now occupied the entire island site surrounded by Leadenhall Street, Lime Street, Leadenhall Place, and a public path along the west side.

In the last days of 'the India House' its museum collections of Oriental objects, now mostly in the Victoria and Albert Museum, spread throughout the building. Views of 1858 show galleries fitted up by Matthew Digby Wyatt in a Victorian Anglo-Indian style with nothing classical about it. In that year the company's powers were taken over by the Government, the vast empire was no longer to be run by a commercial corporation. For two years East India House was the India Office until in 1860 that was moved to a new-built hotel in Victoria Street nearer to Whitehall and the slowly rising New Government Offices designed by Gilbert Scott with an India Office by Wyatt (who had also been embellishing Brunel's Paddington Station).

This City ground pieced together over the years by the directors of the East India Company to make their desirable island site was in the lifetime of the company built upon and decorated to many designs, by anonymous craftsmen, by Jacobsen of the Steelyard, by Jones of Ranelagh, by Jupp, by Holland, by the Cockerells, by Wilkins, by Wyatt – designs all reverberating, as it were, with undertones of other architecture from Italy and India. By 1860, for those with historical imaginations, this was one of the most evocative sites in England. But look what happened next.

Victorian Redevelopment: East India Avenue and After

In 1861 the old East India House and its site were offered for sale, and acquired by a syndicate that included the entrepreneurial engineer Thomas Brassey and that fortunate architect William Tite (no longer, however, designing buildings so far as we know). In 1862 they had the building demolished and formed an East India House Estate Co. Ltd to take over the site and build offices on it for letting. Very much the spec-built stack of offices it was, twenty-six windows long in front with a series of separate staircase entries, a central entry to blocks behind, and a few reverberations of minimal-palazzo style.

The new treatment of the site did, however, contain one humane old-time City element, the pedestrian way named East India Avenue from the central entry aforesaid to Leadenhall Place, with gates at both ends that were closed at night, and flanked by the pair of rear blocks, each with four separate staircases. All these separate entries and stairs – as if still those of Georgian houses – meant no expenditure on grand lobbies and corridors. On the main gateway from Leadenhall Street was concentrated the only decoration, of a congested style common to lesser entrances in the City. The south gateway

(Above) South gateway to East India Avenue, 1862–1924, looking towards Leadenhall Place and the life of the Market.
(Below) The Leadenhall Street front and Lime Street corner as shown in the *Illustrated London News* in 1866. Compare other views of that corner on pp. 125 and 133, and Rogers's entrance today.

bore a chiming clock said to date from c. 1820 and therefore from East India House; its dial was later translated to Lloyd's Leadenhall Place entrance of the 1920s.

This quiet backwater in its prime, for example in 1873, was peopled by a mixed bag of steamship lines, Bombay agents, colliery owners, tea merchants, ship brokers and at no. 7 still, just, 'Wm Arthur Tite, architect, knt, CB, MP, FRS, FGS, FSA.' Fifty years later, while the future of the site was in the balance, nos. 1–8 East India Avenue (not including the offices facing the street) were a warren of eighty-four tenants, the mixture as before.

During 1922–3 this property was the scene, behind the scenes, of much tiresome manoeuvre. The protagonists were Lord Kylsant (Owen Philipps, first Baron, died 1937), Chairman of the Royal Mail Group of Shipping Companies, and Arthur Lloyd Sturge, Chairman of Lloyd's, and in the background the property company that had taken a long lease on the site just before war broke out in 1914. By the time Lloyd's realized they must absolutely leave the Royal Exchange and that this site offered the space needed, Lord Kylsant had bought a half-interest in it with a view to his own headquarters. This, at that time, preposterous figure, whose business career was to end sadly a few years later, could not make up his mind which part of the site he wanted and which part he would allow Lloyd's to have. The shilly-shallying went on for almost two years, met by Sturge's firmness and patience in the knowledge that such sites were scarce. At the end of 1923 it was agreed, Lloyd's was to have 44,000 square feet at the back, for the Room and offices, a passage through to Leadenhall Street and frontage there of sixty feet for a stately entrance. Their building was to be, as it were, wrapped round two sides of the Royal Mail building, which was to have the Lime Street corner and the lion's share of the Leadenhall Street frontage. Sturge's skill in taking Lloyd's to Lime Street was equal to that of Angerstein when he took Lloyd's to the Royal Exchange a century and a half before.

So East India Avenue was pulled down and the whole site lay open during 1924–5 as it had in 1862. The shallow depth of it, before excavations for basements began, showed how shallow the Victorian and earlier foundations and cellars, if any, had been. After the demolitions and before excavation began, there was a football game, Housebreakers *vs* Navvies. As the Great Fire of 1666 did not come here, the clearances of 1862 and 1924–5 made the first modern clearing of the site, though not the last.

The New Lloyd's Building and the Royal Mail Building

Both these buildings were designed by the same architect, but not, it must be said, with the thought that they might at some future time be united. So when they actually were, certain differences in levels prevented a good union being made of it. Free enterprise operated from the start.

Sir Edwin Cooper, it would appear from the professional journals of the 1920s, was one of the most fashionable architects of big buildings of his day. There was no competition for the Lloyd's building (and there is some evidence that Lord Kylsant had already asked him to design for him), but certain massive works recently completed by Cooper will have lent weight to his appointment: his town halls at Hull and Marylebone, and that showpiece on Tower Hill, the Port of London Authority headquarters. Pevsner in the mid-twentieth century called that 'a lasting monument to Edwardian optimism, like a super-palace for an International Exhibition, showy, happily vulgar, and extremely impressive'. And still today one's reaction on sight of it, whether pro or con, is 'wow!' In 1922 Professor Reilly of Liverpool even said the P.L.A. building explained to him 'why we beat the Germans'. Be that as it may. Cooper's knighthood in 1924 was more especially the result of his designing without fee the Star and Garter Home at Richmond for servicemen disabled in that war. The delay caused by war does explain why some of the showiest buildings of the 1920s were conceived in the Edwardian period. But Lloyd's new building was conceived and produced without delay in the mid-

Building works on the site of East India Avenue in 1925, with the row of shipping offices opposite on the north side of Leadenhall Street, the church of St. Andrew just visible at rear right, and the east side of Lime Street at right.

1920s. Preparations for its companion building were made at the same time, though Lloyd's was to be finished first, in 1928, the Royal Mail being delayed by a shortage of steel after the General Strike of 1926, or so it was said.

Their architect was about fifty when he designed them, with substantial work behind him. Behind him as well was a solid (too-too solid, a later avant garde was to say) body of accumulated classical tradition, still in process of revival for commercial buildings and especially then for railway stations and town halls, not only in Great Britain but also in Europe and America, and everywhere inflated in size, accommodation and cost. It may, incidentally, be noted that when Cooper's generation was young the paintings of Alma-Tadema and Leighton and Poynter presented a world of classical palaces. When the travel writer H.V. Morton said in the *Daily Herald* in 1932 of Lloyd's Room that, emptied of its boxes it would be the kind of place where 'Antony and Cleopatra might have staged one of their Alexandrian indiscretions', one is reminded that Late Victorian painters were creating such stage-sets before Late Edwardian architects did. While the latter were growing up, the art magazines they looked at were full of the former. But there was more to it than that.

When Cooper, a Yorkshireman, became a partner in a practice at Scarborough in the 1890s, early joint works included a college in 'Free Tudor' and a school in 'Queen Anne'. In the new century, however, influences more congenial impelled the powerful design of the Guildhall

Leadenhall Street's new scenery after 1928–9. *(Left)* The Royal Mail Steam Packet Company's bold front and Lime Street corner. *(Right)* Lloyd's comparatively modest entrance at the far end; but see Lloyd's side view on the next page.

and Law Courts at Hull. By the time he had won the St. Marylebone Town Hall competition in 1911 he had moved to London and in the following year he won the Port of London Authority competition. The inflated antique forms of those buildings fitted the taste of the times. Norman Shaw's late Piccadilly Hotel with its giant colonnade and baroque gables had risen in the centre of London, John Burnet had added a brilliantly classical north wing to the British Museum, Mountford had replaced Dance's prison with his own New Bailey as then called, Selfridge's with its steel stanchions cased as stone columns had begun, and a series of lectures delivered at the Royal Academy by Reginald Blomfield had become an influential book, published in 1908 as *The Mistress Art*, explaining with what has been called his usual mixture of persuasiveness and aplomb the moral superiority of classical architecture.

Moral grandeur, despite steel encased as stone, was all very well, but

(Above) Lloyd's tremendous elevations on Leadenhall Place and Lime Street, as drawn in Cooper's office and reproduced in the *Builder*. *(Below)* King George V lays the foundation stone in May 1925.

Cooper had Yorkshire practicality too. Although with certain of his first big commissions he was lucky to be dealing with free-standing sites, his value as handler of intricate crowded sites was to make his name in the City. A headquarters building for Spillers (1922–6, now Inchcape's) in St. Mary Axe showed his skill in fitting in his plan, also the open-top vestibule he was to develop for Lloyd's and the Royal Mail. The demands of a tight site (and, of course, of his client's purse) seemed to clear his mind of an urge for the overpowering sculpture he used at Hull and on Tower Hill. (The P.L.A.'s huge tower itself can be seen only as sculpture, it is so useless except as symbol of a great port defying decline.) Lloyd's was a more businesslike affair on a tight site, no giant columns appeared on this very large building's exterior, and such statuary as it had was not elephantine. Before inflating his scale, Cooper seems to have looked back a little to his eighteenth-century predecessors, to the compact elegance of Chambers (his predecessor as, later on, Treasurer of the Royal Academy) and to Adam's deft planning on tight sites – Blomfield having pointed out that Adam's real quality was in his planning, based on study of Rome. And in 1922 Bolton's great book on Adam's work came out. Cooper had done the obligatory 'study in Italy and France' and his generation were well aware of Beaux-Arts planning too. So what did he do with it?

The controlling factor at the core of the new Lloyd's was as always the Room. The City had many models for the building-type planned around a single space. There was Cooper's own domed rotunda for the P.L.A., 110 feet across and 67 feet high with concentric counters, the whole contained as if in a courtyard like the Reading Room at the British Museum. There were also the more subtly-set spaces of Soane's Bank of England, then under destruction; Gibson's banking hall of 1864 in Bishopsgate for the National Provincial, now National Westminster Bank, with its glass domes; Lutyens's

Ground plan (redrawn) of Lloyd's and the Royal Mail premises as occupied by Lloyd's c. 1948, showing Cooper's clever routing of the main approach to the Room from Leadenhall Street (north at right).

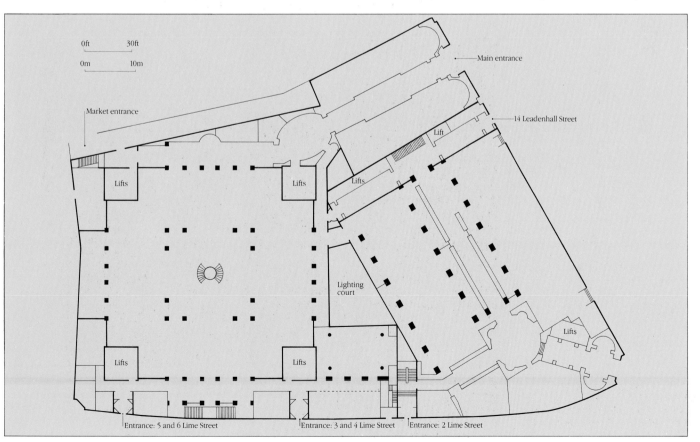

Elevation to Leadenhall Street

These drawings show the grand scale of Cooper's design.

banking halls begun 1924 for the Midland Bank's site running from Poultry to Prince's Street, later to wrap round Cooper's corner building for National Provincial, a less clever building than Lloyd's. And there were the exchanges, the Stock Exchange as it was then, with Allason's timber and glass dome and tunnel vaults of 1853 and Cole's larger dome of 1882, and Bunning's remarkable Coal Exchange opened in 1849 and pulled down in 1962, with its galleried, top-lighted cylinder.

Cooper entirely rethought the old Room at the Royal Exchange: never a centralized space, it had 'just grown'. The new Room was basically a Greek cross, with lift-towers at its re-entrant corners: almost 160 feet across, it was said to be the size of Oxford Circus. Centred on a glass-domed space, it had additional natural light from anteroom windows to Leadenhall Place and Lime Street to south and east, and on the north to a big triangular light well between Lloyd's and the Royal Mail building (a similar anteroom window to the west being filled with Lutyens's war memorial from the Royal Exchange). Viewed from the air, the domed Room seemed a sunken courtyard protected by the ramparts of upper floors (nine storeys above the ground, six above the Room), while to northward the Royal Mail showed great sunken skylights over its booking hall. Only from the air was the hugeness of Lloyd's building, like a liner in dry-dock, fully apparent – Lime Street and its tributary alleys being so narrow – whereas the Royal Mail's main frontage out on Leadenhall Street could be as overbearing as Lord Kylsant might like. So the second architectural challenge Cooper had to meet was the right emphasis for Lloyd's entrance next door.

In a way this entrance bay in its sixty-foot width compared to Kylsant's two hundred-odd was a triumph of English understatement, and Cooper was right not to be florid about it: compared to the Port of London Authority, it was Lloyd's-not-advertising-itself to an elegant degree, yet with a view of receding mountain-ranges of storeys above and behind it. The position was this: Room and Front Door were about 150 feet apart and at an angle to one another. The way between lay along the extreme west flank of the site,

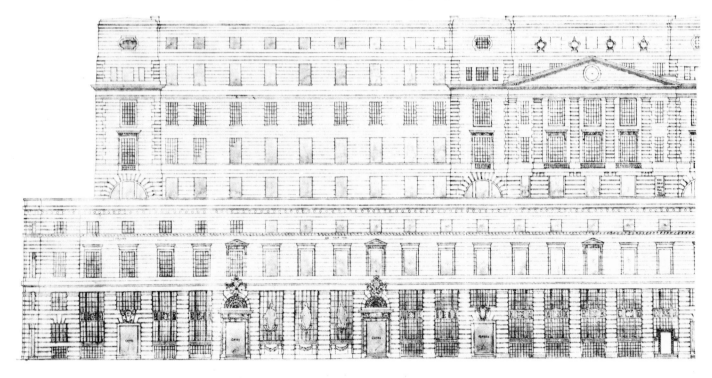

Elevations to Lime Street

Cooper's Design

Contract drawings from Cooper's office (now, Lloyd's Premises Dept). Of special interest is the section at right, showing the Room under its glass dome at the base of a great light-well. Today, Rogers' atrium brings the light-well indoors.

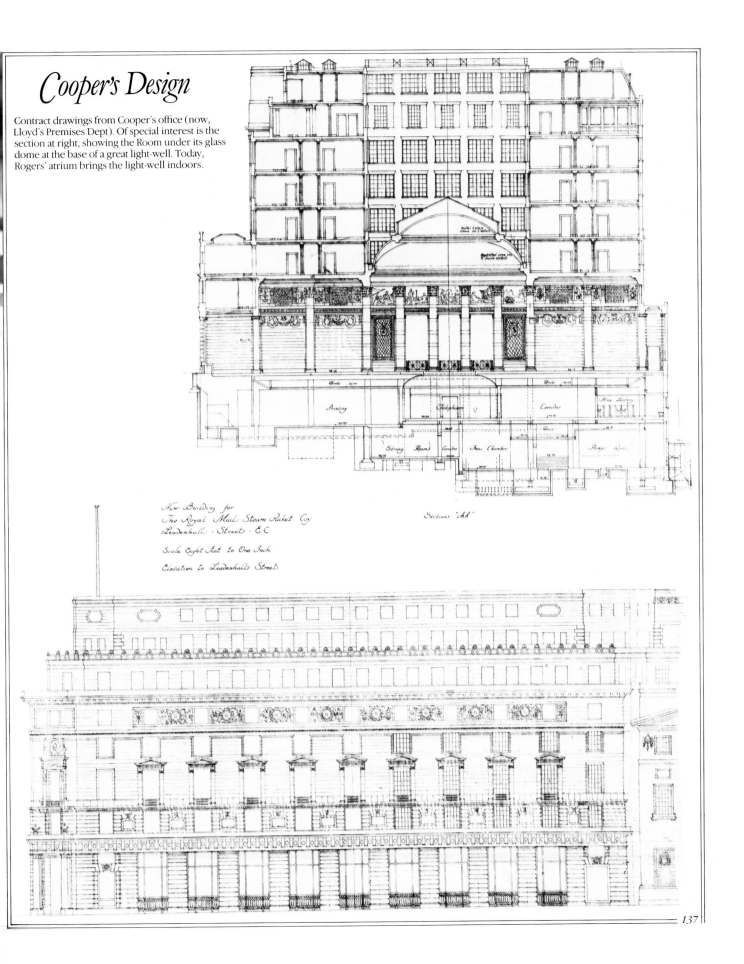

Section "AA"

New Building for
The Royal Mail Steam Packet Co.
Leadenhall Street · EC

Scale Eight Feet to One Inch

Elevation to Leadenhall Street

The Room and its Approaches

(Above) Cooper's Room in action.
(Below) The pivotal elliptical hall on the way in, easing the change in axis of the approach from the main entrance.

(Right) The library, which is being reinstalled in today's building.
(Below left) Cooper's entrance corridor.
(Right) The open well over the elliptical hall.

skirting the Royal Mail's bulk on the east, yet it was no furtive way to the rear, the approach was to be both logical and, within its restrictions, grand. It had four elements: the street door framed in a giant niche centred in a single pedimented bay, a tunnel-vaulted corridor flanked by long narrow bank premises and with its own small dome halfway along, an elliptical hall enabling the necessary change of direction beyond it – the elbow as it were, the necessary pivot or fulcrum that made the whole thing work – and finally the anteroom paralleling the western arm of the Room. As a founder with other architects of the London Society in 1912, Cooper will have been well aware of Georgian town-planning use of circuses and crescents to ease changes in direction.

The entrance front still stands on Leadenhall Street as sole survivor, shorn of the mountain-ranges behind it so lording it less than once it did. The programme for its pediment sculpture was this: at the centre a globe, supported on one side by a female figure (commerce) with a lion for courage and a hive for industry and on the other side by a male figure (shipping) with an owl for wisdom – more or less the message of Jupp's pediment that lorded it over the entrance to East India House, of which the exact site was a few yards along. The message is that of any ancient City site: nabobs come and nabobs go, but business goes on.

Meanwhile, the giant niche as central figure of an urban façade, that is, a piece of street-scenery, appeared spectacularly in 1925 at the foot of Kingsway on the first block of Bush House, Aldwych, by American architects with the verve and finesse of New York big-business classical style. And a New York theatre architect was about to apply the niche feature to the front of the Empire Theatre in Leicester Square. Yet the apse-like front had been neatly done in London, giving depth to a secular-looking church front in Curzon Street, as early as 1910 by Lanchester and Rickards. Cooper in 1924 designed his own quieter version of this unifying feature for the main entrance of Lloyd's, suited to the sidelong views of what was still a narrow built-up street. He may have remembered, too, Jupp's single arched window that unified the Lime Street end of his India House front block, available to Cooper with his interest in the London scene in old prints.

Inside, the importance of his elliptical hall was heightened by the open well in its coffered vault: suddenly uplifting the view after the tunnel vault of the entrance corridor, a favourite neoclassical trick. The colonnaded and balustraded treatment of this opening he apparently adapted from the unique seventeenth-century staircase lantern at Ashburnham House (now part of Westminster School), attributed to the architect John Webb – a feature used in Cooper's youth by Belcher and Pite at the Institute of Chartered Accountants. Cooper used it in circular form over Royal Mail's rotunda-vestibule, as he had for Spiller's in St. Mary Axe. This sudden release from the onward march, this stopping to breathe and look up, meant that the lost vista ahead, with changed direction beyond it, didn't matter. The upper lobby around the open well led to the chairman's office and committee room at mezzanine level.

Cooper's *tour de force* in the Room was the new rostrum. For old-timers it took some getting used to after the homely air of the comparatively diminutive pulpit at the Royal Exchange. Being in the centre and incorporating both bell and clock, this one had to be more than a pulpit. It is a superb piece, like a circular garden temple, and a sophisticated amalgam of sources, based first of all on the fourth-century B.C. monument of Lysicrates in Athens, source of so many tomb and fountain canopies, belfries and follies ever since. The very fact that Lloyd's called this a rostrum, and that the old coffee-house pulpit had been used for ship auctions, could have summoned to the mind of any well-off West End Londoner the auctioneer's rostrum at Tattersall's the famous horse salesroom at Knightsbridge Green, though that

(Opposite) The rostrum of 1928–58, which is being reinstalled in 1986. Cooper's spirited piece is an elongated version of an ancient Greek design adapted to monuments, tombs, follies – and rostrums – of many centuries.

was a simpler Ionic stone affair (perhaps dating from the earliest days of the Greek Revival in the 1760s, when Tattersall's was founded on another site near the Park). But Cooper's tall crowning construction with four-dialed clock was apparently developed from his own centrepiece in the P.L.A. rotunda. Under the canopy was hung the Lutine Bell, and the caller stood below it. Around the base of the rostrum two staircases swirled down to the telephone room in the basement.

The Room was lined with a warm-hued marble. There were bronze and wrought-iron gates and grilles. The central light-fitting had lively metalwork seahorses around its rim. Compared to the fittings then being installed at Selfridge's (such as lift-cages now at the Museum of London) the richness here was restrained. *The Times* even commended the decoration for its 'modesty and light-heartedness'. Ceiling paintings over the side bays included a Tiepolesque 'Neptune and Mercury' panel by William Walcot the extraordinary architect-painter-perspectivist. There were portrait medallions in fibrous-plaster relief on the walls of the Room, the Library had a handsome apse, the Committee Room had walls lined with free-standing columns carved in walnut and furniture designed by the architect, there was stained

Impression of the approach to the new Room in 1928 by William Walcot (1874–1943), one of several perspectives by him published by the *Builder* the week after the formal opening. His dashing style gave a sparkle to Cooper's columns and to sauntering underwriters.
Original drawing, private collection

Sir Edwin Cooper (1874–1942), winner of the Royal Gold Medal for Architecture in 1931.

glass with heraldry and figures of Fortitude and Knowledge. From the Captains' Room upstairs on the sixth floor 'the masts of the ships in the river' could be seen (*Sunday Pictorial*), not that there were sailing masts by then. And in that restaurant, by then Lloyd's own eating-place, the *Evening News* said in 1937, '£500 million worth of insurance sits down to lunch'. Cooper housed them well, as their number stood in 1928. By 1936 it became possible and necessary to overflow into Royal Mail House. The story of the overflow belongs with that of his successor's problems.

When in 1942 Sir Edwin Cooper died in his office at Gray's Inn, he was said to have 'executed more work in the City than any architect since Wren' (*Country Life*) – a statement less accurate in terms of numbers of buildings than in terms of tonnage displacement, to borrow a marine phrase. By 1942 critics were ready to deplore his taste but still admitted that 'he never allowed it to interfere with the convenient planning of his interiors'. It might be true to say that Cooper planned for the convenience of the status quo, tempering with experience the style he had taken hold of with both hands in his Edwardian youth. By the time the Royal Institute of British Architects, of which he had been a Fellow since 1903, awarded him the Royal Gold Medal for Architecture in 1931, the more successful new buildings in England were about to take on a Swedish tinge, and an even more advanced avant garde was about to form.

Cooper was neither the first nor the last recipient of the Royal Gold Medal to be concerned with this site. That is, if we include Charles Robert Cockerell, who assisted his father in the years of his surveyorship to the East India Company, however unkindly that ended in 1824, and who was himself the first recipient of the Royal Gold Medal in 1848. Now the award has come to the site's latest architect in 1985. How many London sites have been mulled over by three Royal Gold Medallists?

Neighbours East of Lime Street before 1941

Until the City's dreadful night of 10 May 1941 a typical cluster of back-street buildings stood opposite Lloyd's mighty flank, on the east side of Lime Street behind Leadenhall Street's rear premises and along Fenchurch Avenue, then only half its present length east-west before turning north for a bit, and along the ins and outs of Billiter Court, Billiter Avenue and the upper west side of Billiter Street. On that terrible night, when Lloyd's with its highly organized A.R.P. came through almost unscathed, nearly all the buildings to eastward were wiped out. None of these mostly four-storey stacks of offices was architecturally notable. There might be one to three offices to a floor on a single staircase, with a housekeeper in the garret. But a little excavation in old directories and landlords' records would show that their miscellaneous occupiers formed a typical slice of the old City of London compost heap: a metaphor more complimentary than it sounds, for business is fertilized by multiple clusters of small offices as well as by a few huge ones. A habitat was wiped out there that night. In 1914, for example, Fenchurch Avenue accommodated ship brokers, engineers, guano and phosphate brokers, ship owners, ship builders, East and West India merchants; and in 1940 a similar mixture much infiltrated by insurance.

In fact, the very first announcement in 1923 of Lloyd's impending move eastward influenced the character of the Leadenhall Street neighbourhood. One chairman of a leading firm of marine underwriters said that within six hours of the news being made public, he had secured the lease of premises in Lime Street. *The Times* exaggerating a bit in 1928 said that once 'the visitor to these street, lanes and alleys would have noticed few names but those of shipping companies. Now the names of leading insurance companies are blazoned on the buildings.' Property owners were grateful to Lloyd's for enhancing the value of their freeholds, more than tenants were during the lean times for shipping people outbid by prosperous marine insurance brokers.

The great site cleared by the Luftwaffe and occupied from the 1950s, as we shall tell, by Lloyd's second new building, had an ancient past, as Dr Harding has told us. Both its southwest corner and most of its northeast corner, together almost half the present site, were until 1951 old possessions of the Fishmongers' Company, the Lime Street piece from 1501, the Billiter Lane (later Billiter Street) piece from 1468. At the rear of both properties, until late in the seventeenth century, there were gardens, forming with neighbouring back gardens a leafy area of private quiet. The Great Fire of 1666 only scorched the edges: the houses of Leadenhall Street, upper Lime Street and upper Billiter Lane were preserved from the flames by their gardens. But by the end of the century the gardens were being built over, their rentability especially for warehouses was too good. Yet still, early in the century, the Fishmongers' Billiter Lane tenant could use a little gate in his garden wall to enter the Lime Street garden, where the southwest corner of

Building works on the new site east of Lime Street in 1952. The huge bulk of 1928 still stands on the west side. The new site included a much older one shown on the opposite page. For its medieval history see pp. 38–41.

the one just met the northeast corner of the other – perhaps (a very rough guess) a few yards east of the Loss Book in the Room of 1958–86.

The post-Fire story of the Fishmongers' Lime Street property is peculiarly interesting because this had long been no ordinary back garden. The houses at the front of the site were let to tenants without use of the large garden lying behind them (roughly 165 feet by 75 feet, or about a third of an acre) which was kept for the private enjoyment of members of the company's court. A long private walk led to it from Lime Street. There were bowling alleys, gravelled walks and a well, there were fruit trees and herbs for company dinners, and there was that civilized bit of medieval garden architecture (periodically rebuilt), a raised gallery or parlour on stilts, large enough for summer dinners – all this because Fishmongers' Hall at the river's edge had no garden. In 1631, while the main medieval mansion facing Lime Street was being rebuilt by a tenant with a long lease, the court rebuilt its gallery along the back wall of one of the houses, facing the garden. The designer was brought in by a friend of theirs in the King's Works office (when Inigo Jones was Surveyor-General) and it is sad that the drawing by

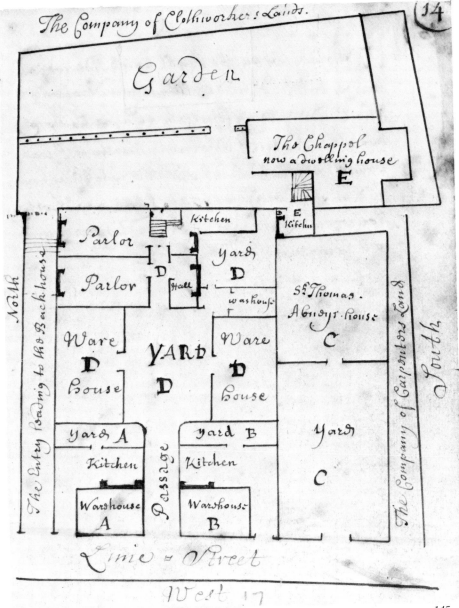

Four houses on the east side of Lime Street as rebuilt in the 1630s. A rough plan of 1721, sketched from a plan of 1686 (north at left). Houses A and B had most of their living quarters upstairs, D was the grandest house. The mysterious 'chapel' in the garden, formerly a summer banquet-room, may have sheltered nonconformist meetings in the troubled 1680s. By 1721 the garden was being built over.

this 'Mr Carter' has not survived. (On the medieval mansion see p. 40.)

All we know of the appearance of this garden gallery – of which the site lies now partly in Fenchurch Avenue, partly under the 1958 Room – is that it was built of stone, about 66 by 20 feet, the main storey 15 feet high standing upon pillars 8 feet high, like a market house on an open ground floor – or like a garden wing at Arundel House modernized by Jones – and that its great room was wainscotted 12 feet high with wainscot pilasters, a plaster frieze above and a plaster fretwork ceiling, and there was a kitchen. For thirty years the new parlour, furnished with tables, stools and cushions, served as an extension to Fishmongers' Hall. But in 1661, feeling poor, the company leased the garden with its parlour altered as a dwelling house. The tenant was Dr Christopher Terne (d. 1673), one of the original Fellows of the Royal Society, whose daughter married the son of Sir Thomas Browne of Norwich, the author of *Religio Medici*. An odd circumstance is that the Fishmongers' private planbook, completed in 1686, labels the great garden room 'Chappel', though it was never called a chapel in the minutebooks. Possibly by arrangement with Terne's widow, court-election services of dissenting complexion may have been held there at a time when religious dissent was not to be flaunted. This private place kept its secrets. It was pulled down in 1735, when the garden itself was already built over, the rearmost ground opened to the east later as Billiter Court.

Of the Fishmongers' four Lime Street houses, three (later nos 45–7) were built as a group in 1631 with and partly over attendant warehouses, the main house lying back and the others facing the street with a courtyard entry between them. These lasted with alterations until demolition in the 1870s, when measured drawings (by the architect R. Phené Spiers) were still able to record interior details of a most retrograde Jacobean style for 1631, compared to a garden house apparently designed by a man from Inigo Jones's office. The rebuilding tenant was prime warden at the time and doubtless building to suit his own elderly taste, while a majority of the court preferred something up to date.

The fourth house, south of the others, was occupied in the eighteenth century by Sir Thomas Abney (d. 1722) though he spent his year as Lord Mayor at Fishmongers' Hall with its grander rooms for entertainment (before there was a Mansion House) and had country houses at Stoke Newington and at Theobalds. The site of this town house, with its warehouse, lies in the roadway of Fenchurch Avenue. Other early eighteenth-century tenants of these Lime Street houses included a Ewer and a Bourdieu, both names that were to appear in the next generation on Lloyd's committee meeting with Robert Adam in the 1770s. By 1811, when no. 46 Lime Street, the main house, still had sixty-odd years to live, it was occupied as ten offices by brokers, merchants and solicitors, with a housekeeper and two occupiers apparently of chambers. After demolition and the eventual formation of part of Fenchurch Avenue, a small office building, no. 47, accommodated a Cape Coast Oilpalm Estate office and various merchants in, e.g. 1914, and various steamship brokers and a shipping line to Morocco in, e.g. 1940.

The Fishmongers' Billiter Street property lies in the parish of St. Katharine Cree, and includes along part of Lloyd's east driveway the site of no. 7 Billiter Street, counting-house and wine vaults of Messrs Ruskin, Telford & Domecq, subtenants from 1815, tenants from 1827, later in the name of John James Ruskin and after him of Peter Domecq. To supplement the records of St. Andrew's parish, which takes in most of Lloyd's ground, it can be mentioned that this ground was left to the Fishmongers' Company by one of its members Henry Jordeyn in 1468. A plan of the site of nos 7, 8 and 9 in 1686 shows three sets of houses and warehouses (including a 'Sugar House') 'promiscuously disposed' as the planmaker patronizingly put it – that is, still in their late-medieval state. The whole site was rebuilt in 1695 with warehouses on the gardens and houses flush with the street. With some Georgian alterations these were what the wine merchant's son, the eminent Victorian John Ruskin remembered:

> His counting-house was a room about fifteen by twenty, including desks for two clerks, and a small cupboard for sherry samples, on the first floor, with a larger room opposite for private polite reception of elegant visitors, or the serving of a chop for himself if he had to stay late in town … The only advertisement … was the brass plate under the bell-handle … businessmen rang the counting-house bell … and were admitted by lifting of latch, manipulated by the head clerk's hand in the counting-house, without stirring from his seat … Billiter Street [was] a narrow trench … admitting the passing each other of two brewers' drays … between three-storied houses of prodigious brickwork, thoroughly well laid.
>
> (*Praeterita* I. vii.153–4)

Lloyd's northeast pedestrian entrance and staircase appear to be on the site of no. 6 (not Fishmonger property). But it was more or less precisely on the site of Lloyd's east driveway exit that early nineteenth-century clients in search of Domecq sherry rang the counting-house bell. Looking into directories of this century, we find an office building called Dock House on the site of nos 7, 8 and 9, its five storeys filled with miscellaneous shipping people in 1940 as in 1914.

These, then, were some of the ghosts among the ruins acquired by Lloyd's east of Lime Street in 1951.

Looking north, with Lloyd's 1928 building at left, the 1958 building before us, and the bridge between them over Lime Street.

A Newer Lloyd's Building

The ceremony opening the next Lloyd's building in November 1957, it was thought at the time, would be seen by later generations 'as the culminating point . . . at which the problem of accommodating the largest insurance market in the world was finally settled'. To review the old, old problem we return to 1936 when Royal Mail House was taken over by Lloyd's (Lord Kylsant's parent company being in liquidation) to extend the previous 'final solution' designed by Cooper only a dozen years before. In the ten years following the opening of the Room in 1928 the number of underwriters so greatly increased that in December 1937 an annexe for brokers was opened next door with a new corridor to it, an amplifier for the caller's voice, and some relief for the new inmates from the turmoil of the Room. Then came the turmoil of war, far more disruptive in the City than the one called the Great War had been, all the horror of that having been across the Channel.

After Munich in 1938 shelters were prepared for the 3700 occupants of the two buildings. Basement corridors were reinforced, escape shafts were inserted, and a bomb-proof shelter in which underwriting could be carried on was built in the sub-basement of Royal Mail House, with telephones and electric generators for light, heat, ventilation, printing machinery, and motors of fire pumps, and with desks doubling as bunks. Other preparations of A.R.P. equipment and water tanks were to be tested to the utmost in 1941. In 1939 provisional arrangements were made to move to Pinewood Studios near Iver in Buckinghamshire if the City became impossible, and certain clerical offices did eventually move out there, with vans going back and forth all during the war. If Lloyd's did become untenable, there was even talk of

Ground plan of the Room of 1958–86, its southern edge formed by Fenchurch Avenue, with Lime Street at left, Billiter Street at right. The site of the Ruskin-Domecq wine office lies approximately in the east driveway exit, upper right.

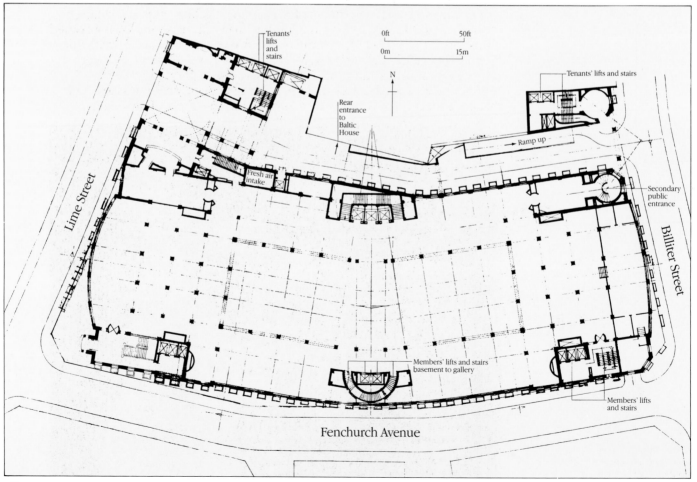

moving the Room to the Egyptian Hall of the Mansion House, supposing that still stood. After war was declared, the 'Casualty Bay' of the Room with its reports of sinkings was screened off with a waiter as sentry and the index of ship movements became top secret under Admiralty control. Yet it was only in Goebbels' imagination that the Lutine Bell 'tolled all day long'.

From 1939 until glass was available again in 1950, the dome over the Room was covered with a non-splintering transparent material. In the post-war gloom of the hard winter of 1946–7 the only artificial light was emergency lighting at the boxes, and the lifts were out of order. Even in 1946, though, the big future issue was seen to be the overcrowding of the Room. The question was soon seen to be, not only how to expand the Room itself into the Royal Mail booking halls, in spite of different ceiling heights, but the future development of the entire premises (space for staff, records, printing, Captains' Room in relation to useful rents from tenants). In early views of the Room in 1928 the space around the boxes looked vast, the ratio of seating to gangways being 1:2, reduced by 1948 to 2:3 – and of course photographs of the unoccupied Room are always unrealistic compared to those of the Room in action. To construct one large Room over the whole ground floor of the two buildings, with the rostrum in the triangular light-well space in between glazed over, would not seat the number then wanting it, quite apart from the architectural problems of merging the two buildings. And Royal Mail Lines still held a lease on part of theirs.

A solution seriously considered was to add a gallery to the Room on all four sides, giving more space without interfering with the domed central space: the Room was barely high enough to take it, especially with the insertion of electrical services under the new floors, and to complicate matters the Royal Mail booking hall already had a gallery at quite a different level. No possible merger would make one magnificent Room. Even a domed ellipse set into the light well would not unify the spaces so at odds with one another – it was almost as if Lord Kylsant were still around. Still, working drawings and consultations with authorities were begun in 1948, all rebuilding having to be licensed. And so matters stood until it was learned that the collection of bombed sites east of Lime Street, gradually being

Her Majesty the Queen laying the foundation stone in November 1952.

assembled into one package by a property company, might become available. In June 1950 it was publicly announced that Lloyd's were negotiating for the whole site. In 1951 town-planning permission and new-building license were received, the more promptly, in this time of shortages of materials, because of Lloyd's importance as foreign currency-earner.

In May 1951 Terence Heysham FRIBA, successor to the late Sir Edwin Cooper's practice, who had been looking after Lloyd's architectural problems since 1928, was appointed architect for the new building on the strength of designs prepared by him. In July the drawings and a model were shown to members in the library. Clearance and excavation of the site went on in 1951–2, and in November 1952 the foundation stone was laid by Queen Elizabeth II on the site of the future main Lime Street entrance, in the presence of the Archbishop of Canterbury, the Lord Chancellor, the Prime Minister, foreign ambassadors and the Lord Mayor. That is, symbolic national importance at this time was attached to the ceremony. The future building's

The 1958 building's southwest corner, on part of the Fishmongers' one-time ground (plan, p. 145), with Fenchurch Avenue at right.

appearance had a mixed reception in the press, however. What the press pictures showed, of course, was a building isolated by perspectivist and model-maker, not neighboured by other buildings. And in 1952 there were more frustrated architects ready to run it down than there were other new buildings to compare it with.

Heysham's problems on this site were somewhat different from Cooper's on his. There was no elbowing by a Royal Mail House. This site had streets on three sides; running a private driveway along the fourth or north side, with only subsidiary entrance-outposts beyond that, made it an entirely island site. There was no main thoroughfare on the doorstep for a grand entrance, instead there could be the grandeur of withdrawal from the main road to a private forecourt. The Room had to be a rectangle over three hundred feet long without looking like a railway-station concourse or a football pitch. Here the architect capitalized on the gentle bend in Fenchurch Avenue dictated by the mosaic of ancient property boundaries combined in the site and defining the

The Room, 1958–86, looking towards the rostrum, with the Loss Book left centre, and the busy boxes.

entire south edge of the building. He will have known a well-publicized New York example of this bending a building along a street line, Carrère & Hastings' Standard Oil Building of 1926, following the line of Broadway, most subtly done within its neoclassical elevation. Not that this always happened: there is nothing subtle about the relentless curve of London's Unilever House of 1930 on the Embankment at Blackfriars.

Heysham had more light and air to play with than Cooper had, partly because of height limitations by increasingly careful planning controls. Above the north gallery of the Room is a five-storey block, over the south gallery a two-story block, a short north-south block between divides the Room's light well medially, and to east and west five-storey blocks are set back from Billiter and Lime Streets. A bridge over Lime Street connected the new building with what was now called the Old Building. Heysham punctuated his varying roof heights with towers at the corners, the south towers with relief-panels symbolizing Earth, Air, Fire and Water, by James Woodford, RA. Before summarizing the external character of this building, we might look into the interior.

The Room with its gallery was, at the time it was built, the largest air-conditioned space in the northern hemisphere. The steady hum of the place at its busiest is never a pandemonium. In appearance, Heysham carried on with Cooper's square piers, supporting the gallery proposed for Cooper's Room in 1948. Though it was not possible on this long site to make this a centralized space, amplifiers make the caller audible. Happily it was possible to place the slight bend in the Room's long rectangle just halfway along its length. In front of it the new rostrum was placed, a rectangular cabinet, at first incorporating a showcase for the Lutine Bell flanked by broker-indicator panels. But it was soon seen that this setting for the bell downgraded its traditional importance in a way all too typical of the 1950s. So a twin to its old wrought-iron framework of Royal Exchange days was brought out of store (the twin having held the clock there, the bell's frame being in use to hold the former East India clock at Cooper's Leadenhall Place entrance). So

The architect Heysham's model, 1951.

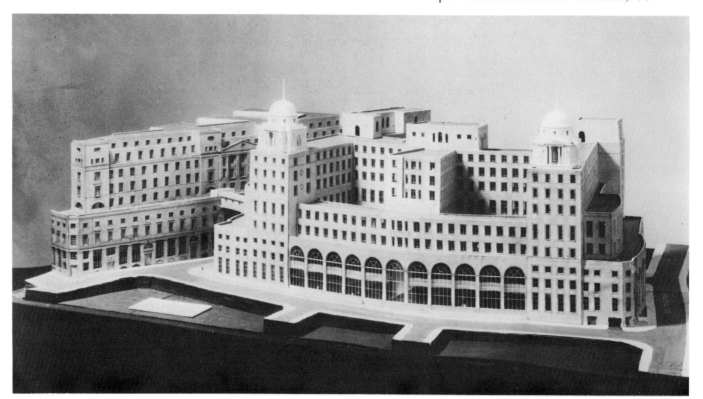

character was reasserted, and the bell made in 1779, among its pleasant curlicues designed in 1897, has spent the years 1958–86 on top of Heysham's rostrum. The ranks of boxes to east and west of it were made to the same basic plan as Lloyd's boxes in action at the Royal Exchange when it was fitted up in 1774 as nearly like the coffee-house boxes of Lombard Street and Pope's Head Alley as possible, and again in 1844 to order, as again in 1928. Only the personal equipment varied: in the 1930s an old hand of Victorian days visiting Leadenhall Street said he saw only tins of sweets where he used to see silver snuff-boxes; now one notices personal computers. Meanwhile, Cooper's circular rostrum, unsuited to any but a centralized space, was retired to store, but Lloyd's treasures first displayed in a Nelson Room set up in the basement of Cooper's building, were newly enshrined in a special room off the west gallery.

Upstairs, Heysham's committee suite was designed around an old room that came to Lloyd's almost by chance. During construction, the architect and the Principal Clerk went, in search of chimneypieces, to a sale of fittings at the Marquis of Lansdowne's great house Bowood in Wiltshire, about to be partly demolished. There they found that an entire room by Robert Adam was available, the so-called Great Room of 1761–4. So they bought its ceiling, frieze and cornice, dado rail, skirting and oak flooring, with certain plaster wall panels, doors and the marble chimneypiece, and reinstalled them at Lloyd's within dimensions considerably adapted from its original setting. This somewhat carefree adaptation, which made it impossible to use the entire ceiling with its original cove in 1958, is being restored nearer to Adam's intentions in the new setting of 1986.

The building was formally opened by Her Majesty the Queen Mother in November 1957. The underwriters moved into it from the older Room, with less nostalgia than thirty years before, at Easter 1958. The old Room, denuded of its *raison d'être* and its focal rostrum, did not lend itself to mixed office uses. It had, after all, been purpose-built. The new Room, like its predecessors, proceeded to operate well for the numbers it had been built

Her Majesty the Queen Mother opening the new building in November 1957.

for, while Lloyd's and its world went on becoming more and more complicated.

Terence Heysham, like Tite and Cooper, was made an honorary member of Lloyd's. He died in 1967 aged 70, less known than they were. His other works in London included rebuilding the Corn Exchange, adding to the Royal College of Physicians, Trafalgar Square, for Canada House, and the medical school at St. Mary's Hospital. His years in Cooper's office had set him in the way of commercial classical revival and, with other such architects feeling the need to make some concession to modernism, he stripped down to a sleeker classicism, as had happened in New York more than twenty years before. Here he was in 1952, smoothing down classical patterns almost to nothing, making those flat arcades of windows on the south side of the Room, applying brief colonnades to the upper storeys of his towers, with acres of featureless fenestration in between and a neo-Georgian porch here and there. Domes he proposed for the towers were averted when critics pointed out the resemblance to Wembley Stadium. Cooper plus H_2O, one is tempted to say, and the *Financial Times* in 1952 was ruder than that, finding it inconceivable that taste had sunk so low. And yet, look at it now, after a walk round the boxier blocks of the new City, take a few turns up and down Billiter Street and note the varied curves of Heysham's setbacks. There is considerable visual relief there, even a certain sculptural quality to mitigate the featureless upper ranges of the building. In the 1950s that was what many a City client was ready for. Yet while Lloyd's building went up, the City's first 'skyscraper' was also going up just around the corner of Cullum Street on the north side of Fenchurch Street, Fountain House, emulating the tower-on-a-horizontal-block of the Lever Building in New York of 1952.

As for the postwar street plan of this neighbourhood, although the lanes and alleys east of Lime Street were wiped out in 1941, the continuation of Fenchurch Avenue kept it narrow, Lime Street is still narrow, and indeed the principal ancient thoroughfares embracing this neighbourhood, Leadenhall Street and Fenchurch Street, are still fairly narrow and long may they be so. The only huge opening up has been on the opposite side of Leadenhall Street, where lanes and alleys that had survived the war succumbed to the plaza surrounding the Commercial Union and the Peninsular & Oriental buildings – insurance and shipping still in charge of that area. In the City of the 1980s, Lloyd's has engendered neither plazas nor boulevards. Its new territory, so far as public shape is concerned, is the skyline.

(Opposite) Air view of the city in the 1970s, looking west along Leadenhall Street, Cornhill, Poultry and Cheapside to St Paul's, with Westminster, the Parks and the Palace in the distance. The whole setting of the book is here: at lower left, St. Dunstan's tower off Great Tower Street, and just right of centre, St. Mary Woolnoth, both the former tower and the latter church as built just after Edward Lloyd's departure from those parishes, at right the Royal Exchange as finished 1844, at lower right Lloyd's 1928 and 1958 buildings as they stood together until 1980. And at upper left the source of it all, the River Thames.

(Right) Postwar street plan showing how Leadenhall, Fenchurch, Lime and Billiter Streets still pursue their ancient paths.

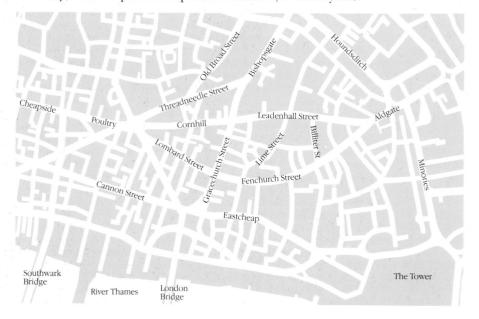

Chapter Seven
Architecture
in Lime Street
today

The new Leadenhall Street profile, with Cooper's grand entrance at right reduced to the scale of postern gate *cum* cat-door.

Chapter Seven
Architecture
in Lime Street
today

In this narrative there occurs now and then the word style, meaning the language of form an architect has drawn upon as if on a deposit account in a familiar currency at a bank. There is no need for the word in this last chapter, there is no controlling language of architectural forms in the last quarter of the twentieth century. The reductions of Mies are past, and the controlling factor is, more than ever, the programme, beginning with the client's recognition of problems and ending with the architect's solutions. The little extra factor one might call, at present, the individual architect's disposition-to-form. It leads in this instance to a busyness of skyline and elevation, and to external surfaces of a medieval complexity – or, of the Cubism of Léger – but raised to a heroic scale on a building one writer calls a magnificent monster and others liken to oil-rigs.

As usual in such matters one must begin with prosaic problems – prosaic but urgent, in a place where the daily density, depending on the time of day, is four to eight times the density of an ordinary office. It had begun to be realized in 1948 that the only way to add space to the Room of 1928 was to go upward, by adding a gallery. So the Room of 1958 was given a gallery all round, and that proved to be far from enough. Eventually an annexe to that Room was made in the basement (the Yellow Submarine) and prefabricated offices were added on the roof. But the gallery itself was static, not to be expanded in any direction – being already at the periphery of the site, and the floors above it divided among a series of linked office blocks – without intense disruption to the market.

The Newest Lloyd's Building

So in 1978 a limited competition was held among six firms of architects invited to propose not a design but a strategy for dealing with Lloyd's space problems. Lloyd's earlier architects had all produced inflexible answers:

(Opposite) Asserting the boldness of Lloyd's, the northeast stair turret at the Lime Street corner as seen from St. Mary Axe.

(Right) Artist's impression of part of the administrative area enclosing the Adam room from Bowood.

Rogers's Design

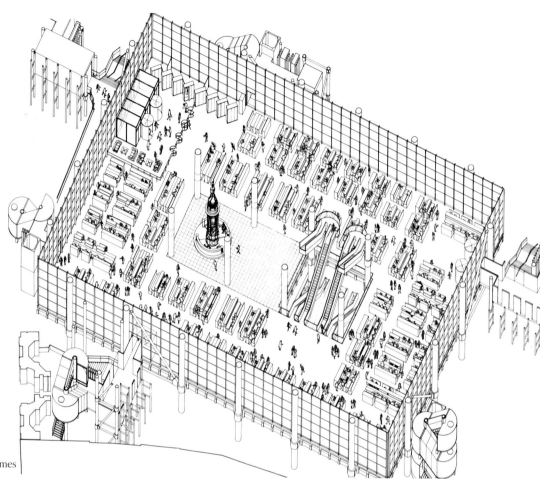

(Right) Diagram of the Room with rostrum, escalators, and boxes.

(Below) The City's graph-paper skyline welcomes Rogers's diagonals.

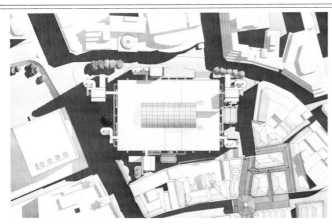

The Room from four points of view. *(Above)* The neighbourhood roof-scheme (north at right). *(Upper right)* Artist's impression of the interior. *(Right)* The vaults of a nave twice as high as Westminster Abbey. *(Below)* Floor-plan (north at left).

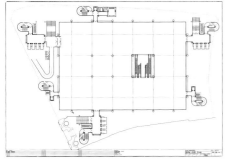

Adam, fruitlessly, in 1772; Tite, for whom Lloyd's was only a favoured tenant, in 1842; Cooper, who also had Lord Kylsant to cope with, in 1924; and in 1951 Cooper's successor Heysham, who had the freedom of his site but was limited in other ways. The winner in 1978 was the strategist who seemed most concerned for flexibility, Richard Rogers. With his partners John Young and Marco Goldschmied and with the client's own redevelopment committee, Rogers worked out his solution for redeveloping Cooper's site on the west side of Lime Street, leaving Heysham's site on the east side of Lime Street alone – the first time ever that the old East India site has been rebuilt all at one go as one single block, rather than the accretions of East India House, the three blocks of the 1860s, or the two of the 1920s, and without even a light well.

For all the seeming complexity of Rogers's building at first sight, the solution is brilliantly simple. The basic element that is new here is an old one raised to new heights, made possible by recent advances in technology and made much of by architects recently: the atrium. The atrium of a Roman house was an inner court open to the sky, an atrium in the middle ages could be a colonnaded courtyard in front of a church. The Crystal Palace showed how such spaces could be glassed over. Indeed, the Royal Exchange courtyard, both before and after it was glazed, could be called an atrium. And the late lamented Coal Exchange was a galleried, skylighted atrium space. But only now when heating and air-conditioning systems have learnt how to deal with an enclosed air space as tall as a tall building, can an atrium be inserted into a skyscraper without being sunk at the bottom of a light well. Marrying the idea of successive galleries over the four sides of the Room to the idea of an atrium over its centre was the core of Rogers' conception. And then he pulled all circulation – stair towers and lifts of half a dozen varieties – and lavatory arrangements to the perimeter of the site, large deliveries and removals to basements, and even the Captains' Room to a lower ground floor, in order to realize the largest possible Room on the main ground floor. The ground-floor plan of this sophisticated building is an unbelievably simple undivided rectangle. Escalators within it bring the first four gallery levels into use as part of that ground-floor level, while further levels above can be let to tenants, glassed off from the atrium, until needed. Cooper's elegant rostrum with the Lutine Bell restored to it stands as focal point of the Room with the atrium's curved roof – like that of the Crystal Palace main transept – more than two hundred feet above it.

The elevation is hard to describe, in extreme contrast to the Commercial Union's mirroring face – reflecting the new building with changing light and clouds – over the way. Lloyd's is mainly twelve storeys high but with taller elements – the arched atrium roof, three 'high-plant' cabins, and the six stair and lift turrets – while the upper storeys in part step down at the rear. There is no leisurely diagonal line of outside escalator as on Rogers's Beaubourg Centre, a building that serves leisure, offering the public a slow view of Paris as part of the building's performance. At Lloyd's the great mass is contained by its individual turrets, somewhat in the manner of Street's Law Courts in the Strand, a comparison Rogers himself makes. But Lloyd's vertical elements are part of a mass of exposed structure and services, a complexity by which the simplicity inside is achieved.

Every floor and ceiling inside, it is true, is stuffed with a spaghetti of services, e.g. for data transmission – today's equivalent of Hozier's signal stations and speaking tubes – and elaborate heat, light and air systems. But the spaces themselves (not yet populated as we write) are uncluttered. The triple skin of the building is mainly of glass, much of it translucent rather than transparent, its surface beaded to give a minor glitter to the light.

Very much more could be said, and is being said, and will be said, in the professional press and throughout 'the media' as these works are completed.

(Opposite) Where Cooper's foothills used to rise behind his grand entrance, a Himalayan cliff-face studded with mod cons.

What we shall all want to know is *how* it works. It is an extremely sophisticated, yet pioneering building. Lloyd's with their worldwide venturesomeness and large sense of their own powers were the right clients for it. Like Concorde, and the QE2, and the Woolwich Tide Barrier, it is a great thing for this country to be doing. During a time of recession in the construction industry this has been the prime building site in the country. An assessment of its performance, and ultimate effect on the client, in (say) the year 2000 must be awaited with interest.

Meanwhile there remains that question of character *vs* environment.

The Character of the Room

All down the history of Lloyd's, said the historian thirty years ago, we saw 'environment working on character'. Yes, even a very tough organism is conditioned by its container. But if the organism changes its container and can make certain conditions for its form, character can work on environment. In each new edition of the Room we have seen the tenacious clinging to box-seating: the table-flanked-by-high-backed-benches formation first noted in London coffee houses at the beginning of the eighteenth century. The box has been the market stall of the insurance market, the basis of the spontaneity of Lloyd's business, conditioning the way it operates. The box in action is the condition Lloyd's architects always have to accept. Every time, so far as property boundaries allow, it is the building that has to give. The success of the latest container will be judged by its flexibility in allowing the boxes – that is, business – to operate, to be serviced, to multiply. The new building has significance for the future of architecture far beyond the bounds of the City. But the Room still has its boxes.

(Opposite) Lloyd's 'large sense of their own powers' expressed in steel and glass.

(Below) The modern version of the box (shown minus benches but with foot-rests), about to be fitted with the latest communications technology, ready to deal with the world.

Index

Acknowledgements

Both authors wish to thank the staffs of the Prints and Maps Section of Guildhall Library, the India Office Library, and Theo Hodges Graphic Design for their assistance. For Part I, Vanessa Harding would like to thank the librarians and archivists of the Corporation of London Records Office, the Manuscripts Section of Guildhall Library, and the Institute of Historical Research, and former colleagues at the Museum of London and the Department of Urban Archaeology. She is especially grateful to Caroline Barron, Martha Carlin, Charlotte Harding, Derek Keene, and John McCusker for their valuable comments and John Meek for his charts and maps.

For Part II, Priscilla Metcalf is most grateful to Lloyd's own Library, Information, Premises, and Secretarial Departments and Redevelopment Office for enthusiastically providing materials and knowledge. In 1984 it was a privilege to be able to talk to Mr Raymond Porter, senior underwriting consultant with experience of The Room since 1912. Especial thanks are also due to the Mercers' Company Archivist for access to records of the Joint Grand Gresham Committee for the Royal Exchange, and to the company for permission to reproduce drawings; and to Sir John Soane's Museum for the opportunity to study and reproduce five drawings by Robert Adam. Richard Rogers' office was helpful with information. We much appreciate Mr Granville-Grossman's willingness to let us show a drawing in his possession, and that of the Fishmongers' Company to show a plan from their records. Many thanks are due to Sir James Richards for reading Part II in proof, and to Jean Imray for news of Adam's work in Frederick's Place.

Bibliography and Sources

Part I. The account of Roman London is based on P. Marsden, *Roman London* (1981), and recent excavation reports and other information supplied by the Department of Urban Archaeology at the Museum of London. The history of the site in the medieval and early modern period is based on contemporary manuscript sources, of the kinds discussed in D. Keene and V. Harding, *A survey of documentary sources for property holding in London before the Great Fire* (London Record Society 22, 1985). See also C. N. L. Brooke and G. Keir, *London 800–1216, the shaping of a city* (1975); John Stow, *A Survey of London,* ed. C. L. Kingsford (1908, reprinted 1971); Betty R. Masters, *The Public markets of the City of London surveyed by William Leybourn in 1677* (London Topographical Society 117, 1974); W. Foster, *East India House, its history and associations* (1924). Professor John McCusker discusses Edward Lloyd's newspaper and the origins of *Lloyd's List* in *The Library: transactions of the Bibliographical Society* (forthcoming, 1986) and more fully in his *European bills of Entry and Marine Lists: Early Commercial Publications and the origins of the Business Press* (Cambridge, Mass.: Harvard University Library, 1985).

Part II. These chapters are based partly on Lloyd's minutebooks, deeds, plans, photographs, reports, commemorative material, scrapbooks of cuttings from *Lloyd's List* and London newspapers, and the following books: W. R. Dawson, *Treasures of Lloyd's* (4th ed. 1930, annotated copy in Lloyd's library); G. J. Emanuel, *Memories of Lloyd's 1890–1937* (n.d.); and the histories of Lloyd's by Wright & Fayle (1928) and D. E. W. Gibb (1958). Adam's drawings for Lloyd's at the Soane Museum have not so far been published in depth. The Royal Exchange chapter is based partly on Gresham Committee minutes and architects' drawings held by the Mercers' Company. For building works from the 1840s to the 1980s, the R.I.B.A. Library's array of periodicals has supplied contemporary comment. Other useful books include: Foster on East India House cited above; H.M. Colvin, *Biographical Dictionary of British Architects* (1978); N. Pevsner, *History of Building Types* (1976); R. Macleod, *Style and Society* (1971); R. Saxon, *Atrium Buildings* (1983). For more on the Fishmongers' garden at Lime Street, see Metcalf, *The Halls of the Fishmongers' Company* (1977), and on interiors of 1631 there, G. H. Birch & R. Phené Spiers, *Nos 45–8 Lime Street* (1875, large pamphlet in Lime Street file, National Monuments Record).

Picture credits

The assistance of the following organisations and individuals is gratefully acknowledged: Aerofilms page 155; British Library 77b, 124, 125, 127t, 130; British Museum 17tl, 18m, 123tl; Corporation of London Records Office 21, 22t, 54b, 55, 58, 74; Peter Cook 158, 163; John Donant 156–165; Mary Evans Picture Library 18t, 34t, 54tl; Fotomas Index 76; Guildhall 14, 18b, 22b, 24, 25, 34b, 35, 37, 39, 40, 41, 42–3, 44, 47, 48tl, 48tr, 48br, 49, 50, 51, 52t, 53t, 54tr, 56, 57, 59, 60, 61, 62, 63, 64, 65, 66, 67, 68, 70–1, 72, 73, 82–3, 94, 97b, 102, 110, 126t, 126b, 127b, 128t, 128b, 131b, 134b, 135, 145; Hulton Picture Library 23ml, 26tr, 26b, 33tr, 33b, 77tl, 87, 89t, 96, 107t, 107m, 107br, 118t, 118b, 118, 119; Magdalene College, Cambridge 11, Mansell Collection 23tr, 26tl, 97t, 120–1; Mercer's Company Archive 98t, 98b, 99, 111,; Museum of London 8, 12–13, 15, 16, 17t, 18t, 19, 20, 26m, 46, 93; National Maritime Museum 122; National Monuments Record 48m; National Portrait Gallery 84; PhotoSource 109t, 114bl, 153; Public Records Office 79; Ronald Sheridan 15; Brian Shuel 48bl; Soane Museum 86, 87; Topham Library 106 (Kodak Museum) 107bl, 117t, 149, 152. Additional pictures supplied by Lloyds Information Department and Paul Dalton. Heraldic drawings by Kate Simunek. Additional picture research by Diana Phillips.